THE WAY TO
INNER PEACE

THE WAY TO INNER PEACE

Finding the Essence of DAO
Through the Sayings of Zhuangzi

by ZHUANGZI
Selection and Commentary by CHEN YINCH
Translated by TONY BLISHEN

SCPG

Contents

Dates of the Chinese Dynasties

Index to Chapters of *Zhuangzi*

Translator's Note
Dao (道) and the Way

Dao (道) and the Way are central to the author's translated text. Bearing in mind that one of the functions of a translator is to support the purposes of the author, this note attempts to provide a brief overview for the reader and in particular to provide a basis of knowledge for an informed understanding of the author's crucial preface.

The meaning and significance of the Chinese character *Dao* is something that almost every translator has to struggle with. Like many characters it is a kind of intellectual shorthand that embodies a number of meanings, many acquired through a process of accretion over at least 2,000 years. Its exact meaning is often difficult to pin down and changes with context. It is easier to describe than to define.

The basic and earliest meaning of *Dao* is "path" or "pathway" and thus by extension "Way." It was used by the early Chinese philosophers, particularly those of the period of the Spring and Autumn Annals and Warring States (770–221 BC) to signify a range of doctrinal concepts and ethical and spiritual constructs extending from the cosmic to the individual.

For Confucius (551–479 BC), who was primarily interested in the human qualities required for good governance and who earned his living as an adviser to heads of state, it was a kind of Grand Principle that stood at the head of a hierarchy of desirable attributes such as humanity, loyalty, integrity, and virtue. Nevertheless, as the author points out, "The 'Way' originally had many interpretations and each sage had his own." In essence, the Confucian Way was a Way of behavior.

The Way of the Daoists was not the same in precise purpose as the Way of the Confucians. It was more cosmographic and took more account of the operation and rhythm of the entirety of the natural world and the phenomenon of change as represented, for example, by the seasons, together with the relationship of all this to man's inner mind. The Way of the Daoists was a Way of existence and of inner being and of action and non-action. Zhuangzi's status amidst the differing Ways of his chaotic times is well described by the author in his preface.

2,500 years on, the major Chinese online encyclopedia entry for *Dao* runs to 17 sections; at its head is the description "*Dao* is a term used by the Chinese people to indicate their self-awareness of nature, meaning the orbit and track of all being and all matter, it may also be taken to mean the operation of change in being and matter." Less ambitious dictionaries suggest "principle," "truth," "morality," and "reason," "skill," "method." The context should indicate which of these is the most appropriate.

Tony Blishen

Preface

Wandering at Will in a World in Chaos: the Spiritual Orientation of Zhuangzi

The social order and cultural concepts established during the early Western Zhou dynasty (1046–771 BC) underwent enormous changes during the period of the Spring and Autumn Annals and Warring States. As Confucius saw it, the circumstances of the "collapse of ceremony and ruin of music" required the re-establishment of order. His proposals were for a return to something of which he approved, the "Rites of Zhou," the Zhou system and culture. Other thinkers, however, envisaged the erection of a new kind of social and cultural order on the ruins of the time. Subsequently, the individual voices of Confucians, Mohists, Daoists and Legalists were all raised in argument and advocacy, becoming what was known by later generations as "the contention of 100 schools."

Zhuangzi (c. 369–c. 286 BC) stood at the margin of the turbulence of real power and intellectual trends, and at the very furthest edge of the restless agitation of actual and intellectual structures.

According to the Western Han dynasty (202 BC–AD 8) historian Sima Qian (c.145 or 135 BC–?), Laozi, the founding figure of Daoism and of an earlier generation than Zhuangzi, was a historian in the Collections Bureau of the Eastern Zhou dynasty (770–256 BC) who controlled rich collections of documents, studied records intensively and from a position of superiority spread his own views, lecturing rulers on how they should handle affairs and conduct administration. Confucius cherished an ambition to save the world; the failure of his official career in the state of Lu was no barrier to his peregrinations through the vassal states, powerfully propagating his views on the restoration of the Rites of Zhou. Mengzi (Mencius) (c. 372–c. 289 BC) followed the example of Confucius and led his band of disciples round the vassal princes eloquently proclaiming "government through humanity (*ren*)." The Legalists, however, set about practical government, employing a set of political stratagems and enacting a complete code of regulations that became the ruling ideology of the state of Qin, the state that united China.

Zhuangzi, however, was very different. To the end of his life, he never possessed any strong inclination to throw himself into actual events. The *Records of the Historian* note that he was an official of the Lacquer Garden. However, we can leaf through the whole of *Zhuangzi* and find almost no trace of this, and in the view of subsequent generations he was more or less reckoned to be a hermit. Zhuangzi did meet a number of powerful figures, such as the King of Wei and his own friend Huizi, minister of one of the states, but his visits seemed neither for peddling his own scholastic propositions nor for the sake of flattery in the hope of worldly advantage. Rather, they appeared to be especially for the purpose of quarrelling and verbal abuse. He did once have a chance of grand office but firmly refused the invitation of the King of Chu. Why was this? It was based on Zhuangzi's strong feeling that his age was one of a "world in chaos." Later, Zhuge Liang (181–234), the late Han dynasty military strategist, remarked in his *Scheme for the Dispatch of Armies* (*Chushi Biao*) that: "If you wish to survive in troubled times, do not seek fame amongst princes." This should stand as the principle upon which Zhuangzi confronted the real world.

In opposition to the concern of many thinkers of the time for "all under heaven," Zhuangzi was concerned most of all for a grasp of the individual self. His *Treatise upon the Ordering of Things* chapter even reveals his weary boredom with the arrogant discourse of the various sages. Zhuangzi certainly considered that he could only control what he was able to control, his own living and life. He ensured that he was able to continue to live under such serious circumstances, even in deprived surroundings, by making straw sandals for a living, and he studied how to concentrate the mind through meditation, causing his mind to become as clear and tranquil as a mirror. He often penetrated the hills and forests, fishing at the water's edge and talking of irrelevant trivialities with close friends, sometimes revisiting old arguments, but the subject of discussion was absolutely not how to govern the world but rather … "are fish happy to swim?"

However, if it were just like this, then Zhuangzi would merely be an ordinary person with a few limitations. The historian Sima Qian said of him: "There is nothing into which his learning does not enquire." With superior learning and knowledge, Zhuangzi not only carried the direction his own self followed into daily life but also towards a transcendental spiritual ascent and freedom.

Zhuangzi's vision was not confined to the actual mundane world, the scope of his life lay more and more within the natural world, and his inner mind extended to include not only the world of man but all earth, oceans and sky, where trees and plants flourished, birds flew, and animals roamed. The graphic image of the *kunpeng* bird spreading its wings in the opening of *Wandering at Will* is an illustration of this, utterly different from the people-populated scenes of the opening of the *Analects* or *Mengzi*. Even in Zhuangzi's eyes, however, the great *kunpeng* bird, spiraling upwards and then soaring 900,000 *li* southwards, is of limited existence. Zhuangzi's *Wandering at Will* is a solemn contract with the Way of the natural world. This is most clearly expressed in his comments in the *Beneath Heaven* chapter: "Associate only with the spirit of heaven and earth." In the intellectual world of ancient China, all sentient beings including man owed their existence to the gift of heaven, heaven was the original source of man, and the basis of his significance and value. Hence, in Zhuangzi's mind, it was only by returning to the very basis of the spirit of heaven and earth that man could attain true, carefree "Wandering at Will."

Only through an ascent to the realm of heaven and earth is it possible to perceive what is large and what is small, what is a senselessness unworthy of attachment and what is truly important. Like the great *peng* bird looking down as it soars the high heavens, the *Floods of Autumn* chapter sighs: "Between heaven and earth I am like a pebble or plant on a huge mountain ... the states of the center amidst the seas, do they not resemble a grain of rice in a granary?" Hence, everything for which man struggles day and night in the world, appears pathetic, and the various disputes between people appear limited and superficial.

It is probably in this sense that the *Treatise upon the Ordering of Things* expresses indifference and detachment about the multifold differences and distinctions of the things of the world, preferring to wait until they were categorized before viewing. Zhuangzi could not fail to take account of differences nor totally wipe them out. The different paths of life are a matter of individual choice. Profit and loss, right and wrong are, in the end, responsibilities of the self and Zhuangzi was unwilling, disdainful and had no need to descend into senseless dispute. Within this reluctance to become involved in senseless dispute there was pity and even sympathy for the people and things of the world.

In reality, Zhuangzi harbored true sympathy for all the various diverse strands of the world and even if heaven and earth already contained differences, all living things originated in the nature of heaven and earth and each had its reason for growth and existence. Consequently, Zhuangzi's fundamental attitude towards living things was one of respect for the fact that they had all derived from the original natural state of heaven and earth. For example, a human life of 100 years had a beginning and an end, this was a pre-ordained natural process, so one should live one's allotted lifespan fully and when returning to earth calmly await the dispositions of time. Take the beauty of the things of the world, for example the trees with which Zhuangzi was so familiar, their slanting natural growth had no need to conform to the worldly utility of building houses or furniture, no need to undergo the beauty of carving or decorating; as for political order, one should respect the natural nature of those who organized society and use that nature as a standard for plans and programs.

At the time, there were probably few people who listened to what Zhuangzi had to say and fewer still who acted upon it. However, the faint voice of Laozi saying "Weakness overcomes strength" became more and more distinct, entering the inner mind of man as generations passed and becoming an important, even indispensable, source of spirituality. Zhuangzi showed people how to preserve one's self in difficult situations and survive in times of hardship and how to raise one's own spiritual state; how to rise above the clamor of opinions and how to refute them; and amidst the unending confusion of the ways of the world, how to cherish emotional richness and a free spirit.

Chen Yinchi

The soul of man is more spacious than the heavens

In the oceans of the north there is a fish called a *kun*. Nobody knows for how many thousands of *li* it extends. Turned into a bird it is called a *peng* and nobody knows for how many thousands of *li* its spine extends. When it takes flight, its wings resemble the clouds at the edge of heaven. When the sea is rough this bird removes itself to the southern seas. The seas of the south are a heavenly pond. In the *Qixie*, a record of curiosities, it is said: "When the *peng* moves to the southern seas it fights its way through 3,000 *li* of water and then spirals aloft 90,000 *li* to ride the summer gales." (*Wandering at Will*)

Nowadays, when we wish people a bright future, we often quote sayings such as "the *kunpeng* spreads its wings" or "the *peng* journeys 10,000 *li*." Their origins lie in the very beginning of the *Xiaoyaoyou* (*Wandering at Will*), the first section of Zhuangzi's works; open it and they instantly strike the eye. This passage fascinates us, mostly because it reveals a realm of huge extent: imagine how vast the space must be in which this enormous thousand *li* *kunpeng* can hurtle across 90,000 *li* of distance.

However, in reality, it is just not possible that an animal of these dimensions could exist, whether fish or bird; nor can there be an altitude of 90,000 *li*, it would be far beyond the atmosphere and the *kunpeng* would have difficulty in breathing, seeing and hearing. This being so, what can be the significance of this opening passage?

Since it is an unreal situation, we should say that it

is, for the most part, a description of a mental state. One feels that along with the altitude of the *kunpeng* one has transcended the ordinary world and escaped the confines of the everyday. This is an enormous expansion of the dimensions of space.

Is this true? Perhaps a response may lie in the words of Victor Hugo: "Oceans are greater than continents and the sky is greater than the oceans, but the soul of man is vaster than the sky." The world of the mind can be enlarged, it is just that the average person has forgotten how to do so.

When you transcend to a higher state, there is no alteration to your fundamental body but its significance is not the same. Zhuangzi tells this fable once recounted by the sage Dai Jinren to the King of Wei: "On the left horn of a very small snail there was a country, and there was another country on its right horn. These two countries fought each other incessantly and many thousands were killed." (*Zeyang*: "The country on the left horn of the snail was named Chu and that on the right was named Man. They waged war over territory all the time, the dead ran into tens of thousands and it was fifteen days before they returned from the pursuit of the defeated enemy.") As the two countries on the snail's horns saw it, what they fought over was vital and they had no qualms in paying a heavy price in lives. However, as we see it, this kind of slaughter is a joke. Why is there this kind of difference? It is because we observe things from a higher viewpoint. For the same reason, were we to observe all the various actions and behavior of constrained humanity from a cosmic point of view on the back of *kunpeng* as it flew through the heavens, would that not be a joke as well?

This is not a step backwards to a chat about the world as it was but rather a new panorama of the mind where "to observe with the vision to see a thousand *li*, you must climb another flight."

Water may support a boat but can also capsize it

If the volume of water is too little, it cannot support a boat. Pour a cup of water into a hollow in the ground, and a blade of grass may make a boat. Put the cup in and it will stick on the bottom because the water is too shallow and the boat is too big. (*Wandering at Will*)

Once it has accumulated the strength to fly the *kunpeng* stretches its wings and ascends "90,000 *li* and with the air beneath it, may ride the wind." The achievements of life are usually gained after much effort and through trial and tribulation; even chance good fortune, such as tripping over a bar of gold in the road, at the very least requires you to step out of the house.

In the events of life, joy and pleasure always come hand in hand with gain and loss. The fable of the 10,000 *li* journey of the *peng* is often taken as a symbol of freedom. However, is not its need to ascend on the wind, in fact a limitation or, rather, a lack of freedom? The *Qixie* says that the *peng* "spirals aloft 90,000 *li* and rides the summer gales." Is the fact that it requires the winds of summer to do so, a freedom or the lack of one? When the cowherd and the weaving maid meet on the magpie bridge across the Milky Way on the 7th day of the 7th month they do so only once a year.

Man suffers more

The morning mushroom that dies in the evening knows not the passage of a day, nor the cicada the passage of a year. (*Wandering at Will*)

In spreading its wings, the *kunpeng* displays the vast realm of the dimensions of space. In the dimension of time, man, according to the two statements above, must break forth from the restrictions of self.

Every being in the world lives in both time and space. The restrictions under which man exists derive from these two states or concepts.

The restrictions of space are relatively straightforward. "Hills outside hills and buildings beyond buildings" suggests that there is another world beyond the one in your field of vision, perhaps the wastes of the north or the Pure Land of Ultimate Bliss of the Buddhists in the west. On the face of it, the restrictions of time are comparatively abstract. The animals of the African savanna are able to comprehend that far away there is a rich pastureland where they can exist and thus migrate thither in haste despite the difficulties and dangers of the terrain. Nevertheless, they may not be aware of the pitiless elapse of time as they move within this space, nor, as they hurry towards new hope of life, that they are also hurrying towards death.

Animals for the most part live in the present, man has a greater sense of time and a greater understanding of its meaning. It is just that people constantly ignore the march of time, especially when young. The less time spent floating in the river of time the easier it is to overlook its existence, in the same way that the morning mushroom and the cicada cannot comprehend the passage of a day or a year. The circumstances of man are actually rather different. It is much the same with the years of a life of a hundred years. However, the older you are, the less time remains, and this in its turn lends a deeper and deeper significance to the phrase "time is short." In all truth, the more you have lost, the more you come to understand.

In this respect, it is man who suffers most of all.

Pride and a tranquil mind

To be praised by all yet not to strive more, to be condemned by all yet not to be despondent, one must determine the difference between internal and external and distinguish the boundary between glory and disgrace. (*Wandering at Will*)

Man lives within society. The Confucian tradition within Chinese culture laid particular emphasis upon the relationship between people: "lords should be lords, ministers should be ministers, fathers should be fathers and sons should be sons" as Confucius put it in the *Analects* (*Zi Lu* chapter), each kind of person playing its own role in society. This naturally has extreme significance and in the end it is only this sort of society that is stable. Nevertheless, the constitution of society is the result of individuals yielding a little of their power in mutual adjustment and curbing their own aspirations, interests and freedom. This has to be so, but it is unfortunate that many people fail to understand this principle and regard the pursuit of external values as their aim, losing their self through "too much is as bad as not enough."

It is at this point that the significance and meaning of Zhuangzi becomes obvious.

The crux lies in "determining the difference between internal and external." Being aware of the difference between what is internal and what is external is extremely important for every individual. Managing interpersonal relationships is partly external, the relationship between self and others, and partly to do with self, distinguishing between the inner mind and the external and thus becoming aware of and maintaining one's own inner requirements and values. The inner self concerns itself with awareness and understanding so that the concepts of glory and disgrace can no longer influence it. Suppose that there was something that everybody was against but it actually suited your own instincts and despite strong opposition you pushed ahead regardless; and suppose there was another set of circumstances where everybody approved, that also would be no matter for complacency and self-congratulation on your part. These two different sets of circumstances arise out of the fact that our conduct is by no means determined by external factors but is rooted in the self. Thus, disapproval and approval can have no influence since they are external factors.

In the secular world this is an extremely elevated condition; the inner mind of those in such a condition is both proud and tranquil.

What are genuine requirements?

The wren nests deep in the forest, it needs no more than a twig upon which to perch; the mole drinks at the stream, it needs its fill and no more. (*Wandering at Will*)

In his *Qiushui—Floods of Autumn* chapter Zhuangzi says that the place that man occupies between heaven and earth is no more than a mere pebble or blade of grass on a mountain ("As we stand between heaven and earth, we are like a small stone or plant on a great mountain"). A blade of grass or a pebble is no more than a pinprick, so minute that it is hardly worth mentioning; thus, the needs of a pebble or blade of grass are smaller still. Perhaps just a dewdrop or a ray of sunshine.

Man's journey on this earth really requires very little indeed; thus, the problem becomes the fact that the demands of the mind are always immense. The ancient kings with their reputed harems of 3,000 beauties included some who suffered a lifetime of misfortune; more recently there have been ladies who have obsessively amassed collections of fashionable shoes but have never tried them on in years.

All they satisfy are fictional cravings and not the real down-to-earth requirements of life. Zhuangzi's standpoint is very close to real life and he speaks the truth. You will only be able to understand and grasp your true needs when you cease the pursuit of things that you do not really require.

To know sufficiency is always a joy. In fact, it is probably very difficult to be happy if you have nothing at all, but the possession of even more than a twig upon which to perch and enough to eat and drink does not necessarily represent even more joy. When people look back upon the small joys of childhood they always discover that there is very little that is built upon the possession of material wealth. The rise in the standard of living in recent years is undeniable but on closer inspection there has been no increase in happiness and perhaps there has been a decline—is not all this a reason?

It is no insult to the cook

Even if the cook ceases to control the kitchen, the master of rites cannot abandon the sacrificial vessels in order to replace him. (*Wandering at Will*)

This quotation is the source of the saying "to abandon the altar to take over the kitchen," attributed to Xu You the celebrated hermit of ancient legend.

At that time, the known Chinese world was ruled by the sage-king Yao and this rule belonged to what the Confucianists believed to be a golden age. However, Yao, for no discernable reason wished that the governance should be handed over to Xu You. Xu You naturally declined but first said flatteringly to Yao: "You govern the world and thus the world is well governed, what need is there for me to succeed you? Do I really need this position?" He then delivered the saying above.

Obviously, Xu You regarded himself as the master of rites and Yao as the cook. Master of rites and cook are two totally different occupations, one is in charge of prayers to the gods during sacrificial ceremonies and the other is in charge of the kitchen. There is a hint of distinctions of status in this: the master of rites has a major role in sacrifices to the ancestors. Perhaps, in this case, "cook" does not mean a person who is generally in charge of the kitchen but ought to mean somebody who, in terms of the ceremonies of sacrifice, just prepares the items to be sacrificed. The difference in status between the two is very clear. Since the position of master of rites is higher than that of cook, it is obvious that hermit Xu You believes himself superior in status to Yao, governor of the world and a man of many achievements. Equally, in the eyes of Zhuangzi, a Daoist who had transcended the world was obviously superior to a Confucian immersed in worldly affairs.

Turning a blind eye and a deaf ear

The sightless cannot see the beauty of patterns, the deaf cannot hear the sound of bells. Can it be that

only the senses of the body may be blind and deaf? The consciousness of the mind can be also! (*Wandering at Will*)

It is only when the five senses operate in co-ordination that we can achieve a correct grasp of the world around us. Defects in one sense or other can cause immense trouble. Loss of sight degrades the perception of space and the world becomes colorless; deafness engulfs the world in a deathly stillness that lacks the sound of birds or wind or the sinuous sounds of music. These are unbearable situations.

Nevertheless, more frightening still and difficult to elicit sympathy for are not defects of form but defects of spirit.

Karl Marx (1818–1883) once said that to the unmusical ear even the most beautiful of music lacked significance. The unmusical ear had no structural problems but for it, music was perhaps worse than for the deaf: the deaf merely could not hear, for them it was just silence but for the unmusical ear it was cacophony and even clamor.

A blockage of spirit can be caused by limitations of knowledge and approaching all the richness of the wide world with a narrowness of experience and then, first from astonishment and then withdrawal, finally isolating the self. Or the blockage may be due to arrogance and self-importance, a belief in one's own righteousness, and a rejection and denial of everything that is different to oneself. The eyes of this sort of person may see other things, his ears may hear different speech but none of this leaves any trace in his mind, it is as if he has never seen or heard a single thing.

There are two sayings that describe this situation: the first, "To see but not perceive" and the second, "Turn a deaf ear."

The flavors of speech

Great wisdom is broad and relaxed, petty knowledge is fragmentary. Great speech blazes, trivial speech chatters on. (*Treatise upon the Ordering of Things*)

In the eyes of Zhuangzi, the age in which he lived was one of disorder and confusion. Society was undergoing violent change and multifarious problems were emerging. As people suffered so they sought salvation. Broadly speaking this is the origin of the so-called "Disputations of One Hundred Schools." It was an age of universal clamor. Each sage had his own intellectual interests. Some, such as the Confucians and Legalists, directly expressed their views on the pressing problems of national planning and the welfare of the people; there were others, like the Mohists and Agriculturalists, who expounded ideas of salvation based upon the viewpoint of a particular occupation; others concentrated upon the problems of personal survival and existence in an age of disorder, like the philosopher Yang Zhu and his adherents; The School of Naturalists (*Yinyang Jia*) devoted itself to knowledge of the natural world and its relationship with the world of man; numerous others like Hui Shi (c. 370–310 BC) and Gongsun Long (c. 320–250 BC) examined the logic of speech.

Zhuangzi naturally had his own perceptions and impressions of the various opinions. Although his criticism above is not aimed at a particular school of thought it is, nevertheless, an excellent general description of the style and flavor of the ideological expression of the sages.

Whilst there were significant problems arising from lofty pronouncements and fine words, there was also an unconscious expansion in the form and manner of philosophical discourse. For example, Mengzi himself admitted, "Am I disputatious? I cannot not be!" (*Mengzi—Tengwengong Part II*). Mengzi was ferocious in his abuse of others, describing them as "with neither father nor lord," ("The fellow Yang Zhu's concern for self has no lord, the fellow Mo's universal love is fatherless.") There was considerable rhetoric at the cost of logic which made a profound impression upon people, a victory of style over content.

As to the chatter of "trivial speech," it exhibits a fragmentary "petty knowledge" that suggests that the School of Logicians should be the target. In his *Tianxia* chapter, Zhuangzi criticizes Hui Shi, the founder of the school, for "talking ceaselessly on and on, thinking he had not said enough." Moreover, the "chattering on" in the quotation above describes Hui Shi's expertise in "scattering ideas amongst the multitude of living things but not knowing if they were satisfied." From the point of view of the Way of heaven and earth, the "fragmentary" of this quotation is absolutely the "exhausted labor of a mosquito or a horsefly."

Although what Zhuangzi says derives from his observation of the ideological arguments of that period, is there, maybe, a universality to it? Similar, exaggerated, or superficial, or fragmentary discourse may reach our modern ears any day of the week.

The tragedy of looking back on the process of life

Once cased in this shape and form we must await our end as life runs its course. We now scatter and now clash with the natural world as our course runs in unstoppable haste, is not this sorrow? We toil in lifelong labor without success, exhausted and knowing no refuge in reason, is not this grief? (*Treatise upon the Ordering of Things*)

An awareness of the limits on life comes to all, sooner or later, intensely or apathetically.

Moreover, Zhuangzi was particularly sensitive to the passage of life and fundamentally regarded life as a process of suffering.

Mankind must accept the hardships of its conflict with the natural world ("We now scatter and now clash with the natural world") not knowing whether, at the very end, we have achieved anything ("We toil in lifelong labor without success"), this is at the level of external fact.

It was suffering at the spiritual level that caused Zhuangzi tremors of soul, seeing his own life swiftly approaching its end and being unable to stop the march of time ("as our course runs in unstoppable haste"), then finally looking back over a lifetime of exhausted suffering and finding it difficult to explain ("exhausted and knowing no refuge in reason").

Exhaustion of body and soul is a feeling and perception of life. People exist among the processes of life. Zhuangzi stands above the ordinary man and is able, in a spiritual sense, to transcend externalities and look back over the passage of life, although what he sees still gives man grief, a grief at a deeper level.

Love them all, including their defects

The Way is hidden by minor successes, true speech is obscured by grandiloquence of utterance. (*Treatise upon the Ordering of Things*)

"True speech is obscured by grandiloquence of utterance" is relatively easy to understand, complicated and flowery utterance always obscures the speech that conveys the true essence of words. At the moment, for example, we are flooded by information and there are words aplenty but how much of it is true? The noise of shouting denies us the calm in which we can hear the sound of truth.

"The Way is hidden by minor successes" requires a little more explanation.

Zhuangzi considered that the Way was a whole in which mankind and all living things lived together in mutual interaction; if one gave prominence to one part, that might be a success in that particular area but might be an injury to the Way as a whole. For example, if you cut down a large tree to make a beam for your house that is obviously good, but what about the adjoining twigs and leaves, they have been discarded and that constitutes an injury. How can that injury not also be an injury to the whole original tree?

Somebody might say that this is disposing of the rubbish and retaining the best. Where is the crime in that? Zhuangzi would take a different view. In his *Floods of Autumn* chapter, he attacks the view that one should only retain that which is proper and abandon the erroneous. His response was: "This is to fail to understand the principle of heaven and earth and of all things, how could only heaven exist and not earth or *Yang* exist but not *Yin*?" The affairs of the world consist of mutually interacting theses and antitheses. "Things exist in mutual opposition and not in mutual absence," there can never be just a single aspect. The great modern Buddhist master Li Shutong's (1880–1942) final testament consisted of just four characters: *bei xin jiao ji*, "grief and joy are as warp and weft." Is not the complete life like this, with joy, and with grief?

Consequently, we must comprehend, confront and achieve a tolerant and sympathetic understanding. Whilst we may like and enjoy the good in somebody, we should also realize that the less good, even evil, aspects of their character are actually a necessary part of their makeup. When in love we often say that we love all of the other person, including their defects. Zhuangzi in love would certainly have thought this way.

Be aware of self, be aware of others

For every being there exists an opposite other and for every being there exists a self. The other may not

perceive but the self is aware. (*Treatise upon the Ordering of Things***)**

"That" and "this," "being/object" and "I" are permanent relative opposites. Normally, people adopting the standpoint of "self" draw a clear distinction between "that" and "this" and "being" and "I." This is an unavoidable situation but Zhuangzi warns that we should be clearly aware of it. As a point of view it is both limited and defective. When seeing things from the standpoint of self, one can never actually comprehend the true situation of the other, though of course one is comparatively clear about one's own situation. This is to say that most people inevitably lack a sense of empathy.

Although we may say that achieving self-understanding is in fact easier said than done, concern about self and knowledge of self are, as it were, in the general run of normality. However, understanding the limits and limitations upon self and coming to tolerate others through a rather wider vision is moral integrity of a higher level. Mengzi once said: "It is only the gentleman who can afford the luxury of virtue without property, ordinary folk lack property and hence lack virtue." (*King Hui of Liang—Vol. I*) What Mengzi calls "property" is a limitation. It is only when people have a definite interest from which they may benefit that they are able to acquire definite beliefs. The extent of the benefit and its location differ. People who differ one from the other occupy different positions and thus differ in belief. It was only the class of what Mengzi termed "gentlemen" that was able to transcend the particular *locus* of class or interest and hold distinct beliefs. These beliefs were all-embracing and took into account as many considerations of community as possible. Consequently, the experience of what the "gentleman" perceived and knew was not confined to the self but extended to a knowledge both of self and of the opposite other.

Zhuangzi urges us to rise above the relative opposites of "I" and "being" and be aware both of self and of the opposite other.

If one were not discussing Zhuangzi

Self has its own judgement of right and wrong, the opposite other also has its own judgement of right and wrong. (*Treatise upon the Ordering of Things*)

People invariably consider themselves right and others wrong, thus each side has its own sense and judgement of what is right or wrong. However, since self and other are mutually opposed, it follows that they will both naturally possess their own sense of right or wrong. Self and other, you and I, are all part of the world in its entirety. What Zhuangzi is saying is that, in fact, we should not each be attached to our own sense of right or wrong, it is, after all, biased and one-sided and continuing the argument will box us in and we will deviate from the Way.

However, Zhuangzi's successors did not always adhere to the results of his painstaking thought, rather they used it as a pretext for establishing their own point of view. Kang Baiqing (1896–1959), the modern poet of the vernacular language who participated in the new literature movement of the early 20th century, attended Peking University and was frequently late for lectures. Ma Xulun (1885–1970), an expert scholar of Zhuangzi, was delivering a lecture on one of Zhuangzi's texts when Kang Baiqing arrived, late as usual. On this occasion, Kang Baiqing burst through the door just as Ma Xulun was in full flow. Unable to bear it any longer, Mr. Ma put down his text and demanded: "What do you mean by this?"

Kang replied briefly: "I live far away."

Mr. Ma's temper flared: "Don't you live in Kingfisher Lane? It's only a street away, you can get there in four or five minutes, how can you call it far?"

Kang replied: "Aren't you lecturing on Zhuangzi, sir? Zhuangzi says: 'Self has its own judgement of right and wrong, the opposite other also has its own judgement of right and wrong.' You believe it near, I consider it far."

Mr. Ma was lost for words and angrily dismissed the class.

Sadly, Mr. Ma was lecturing on Zhuangzi. Had it been Confucius he would have been able to say, as Confucius did as he reproved his disciple Zai Yu (522–458 BC) for sleeping during the day: "You cannot carve rotten wood!" (*Analects— Gongye Chang*)

Follow one's own road

Roads are made by being trodden on, things are named through being spoken of. (*Treatise upon the Ordering of Things*)

The Chinese writer Lu Xun (1881–1936) once notably said: "There were originally no roads, having been much walked, then they appeared." (*Gu Xiang—Ancestral Village*) Zhuangzi had already expressed this meaning in the quotation above.

Nowadays, we have no particular feeling for roads, they stretch on in front of you and even if you were to pull down the shutters and cut yourself off from the world, a road would still be there the moment you opened the door. Nevertheless, these roads were originally not there, they were created through the act of walking.

When we walk on an existing road we are confronted by a problem of choice. The American poet Robert Frost (1874–1963) described in his poem *The Road Not Taken* how, one day, walking through a wood of autumnal yellow he came upon two equally secluded and little-used paths. In the end he chose the quieter of the two. Many years later, he looked back on the choice he had made and realized that it had determined the rest of his life:

> I took the one less traveled by,
> And that has made all the difference.

The choice of actual route influences a poet's feeling about life. True, life's path seems shapeless but on the same principle it also only takes shape after it has been trodden. Moreover, you cannot take a path that has already been trodden by others. Each of us must face up to life, make our own choices and then follow them.

The pleasures of living in the present

**The keeper was feeding his monkeys acorns and said:
"Three in the morning and four at night." The monkeys
were furious. So he said: "All right, four in the morning
and three at night." The monkeys were delighted.
(*Treatise upon the Ordering of Things*)**

There is of course a *continuum* of time that joins the past to
the present but there is also a disconnect, this is normal. It
is the same with expressions of speech. For example: "Three
in the morning and four at night." Nowadays in Chinese it is
taken to mean vacillation and indecision, first one thing then
the other, always changing. Its source is the quotation from
Zhuangzi above. Clearly this was not its original meaning.

Zhuangzi believed that all living things in the world
constituted a single body and were not to be forcibly
divided or split asunder. However, people are never able to
understand this and thus cling stubbornly to one thing or
one side, unable to achieve a completeness of vision that
can encompass the whole. It is the same with the monkeys,
unhappy to hear that there would be an acorn less in the
morning but utterly failing to connect with the fact that
there would be more in the evening; however, when told
that there would be fewer in the evening but more in the
morning their fury turned to delight. When we analyze this
a little we realize that the monkeys perceived only their
immediate advantage. We should not blame them. Basically,
animals live in the present, they have neither a sense of
history nor the ability to plan for the future.

Man and monkeys are closely related and the mistakes of the monkeys are made repeatedly by men. How many people today are there who care only for the present, strive for immediate advantage and lack long-term vision? Both the present and the future have to be experienced, you cannot ignore the future on account of the present; to take an extreme example, it would be like always killing a chicken to get an egg.

Most people do not have completeness of vision but people of sufficient intelligence do; but herein lies a problem—that of mutual accommodation between the two. We can imitate the monkey keeper who through following the aspirations of the monkeys finally achieved precisely the same result: the number of acorns neither increased nor diminished, the only difference being that following the adjustment everybody was happy.

Apart from the joy of the monkeys we also seem to hear the faint laughter of Zhuangzi.

From where do we view the world?

When nothing under heaven is bigger than the tip of a hair of molted fur, then Mount Tai is small; when nothing lives longer than a child that dies early, then the long-lived Peng Zu himself is an infant death. (*Treatise upon the Ordering of Things*)

In pre-Qin times Mount Tai was famous for its height. The

Qin dynasty (221–207 BC) politician Li Si (?–208 BC) said, when offering advice to King of Qin (First Emperor of Qin, 259–210 BC): "Mount Tai does not cede its soil, hence its size; rivers and lakes do not neglect small streams, hence their depth. Rulers should not ignore the common people, hence they may understand virtue." (*Memorial upon the Expulsion of Foreign Influence*). However, for Zhuangzi to say "under heaven" and "Mount Tai is small" is very unusual indeed.

Yet behind this apparently ridiculous conclusion there stands the clarity of Zhuangzi's insight.

Man sees things from a particular standpoint. When we say that ants are small and elephants are large, we are using our own visualization as the standard, something that we normally don't mention, even sometimes forgetting that this mode of expression is built upon a basis of comparison. The particular point that Zhuangzi is making is that since the circumstances existing between things are always described in relative terms, it follows that a different point of view will produce a different perspective and one which may even be absolutely different from our normal impression. The hairs produced by animals in autumn may seem tiny but seen from an even tinier point of view they may appear incomparably large. Mount Tai observed by mankind seems very high, but viewed within the scope of the whole of heaven and earth it is too small to be worth mentioning. Seen from the point of an insect that lives only from dawn to dusk, the life of a child who dies before adulthood is so long that it cannot be imagined. The 800-year-long life of Peng Zu seen in relation to all the many ages of the world is the merest flash of a moment. Hence, although Zhuangzi's statement may be curious, there is a reasoning behind it that warns us that there is nothing in the world that is immutably fixed.

The logic of this concept is clearly displayed in the conversation between Hebo, the Yellow River god, and Beihairuo, the deity of the Northern Ocean in the first chapter of *Floods of Autumn*. Hebo regards himself as vast beyond limit but only comes to realize the true extent of boundlessness on encountering Beihairuo. At this point the vastness of the ocean is obvious; however, Beihairuo points out that compared to heaven and earth he is but a grain of millet in the ocean. The vastness of the ocean is suddenly diminished, the crux lies in this shift of the conceptual basis.

Is there not some enlightenment to be gained from this in our ordinary observation of things and events?

Alone no longer

I live together with heaven and earth, I am at one with all living things. (*Treatise upon the Ordering of Things***)**

The beginnings of the ancient classics are particularly interesting, they give you something of a glimpse of the spiritual world of the time. The Confucian *Analects* start with, "The Master said: 'To study and to put into practice is that not also a pleasure'" (*Xue Erh* chapter), presenting an image of an educator "intelligent and devoted to study" and "unaware of the approach of old age" (*Shu Erh* chapter). The opening chapter of *Mengzi* describes his conversation with King Hui of Liang and prominently figures a Mengzi who has travelled widely in the various states, is skilled in oratory and disputation and vigorously propagates his own political theories. *Zhuangzi* opens with the *kunpeng* bird spreading its wings to display a vast world inhabited not only by man but also by birds, beasts and fish. There are heaven and oceans as well, this is a world that includes everything that exists, not just the world of men.

This too is the world in which we have our being, where all living things exist in diversity, living and growing together and exhibiting their own characteristic sights and sounds. It is in this world that Zhuangzi opens himself to all sight and every sound on a journey through heaven and earth to become one with nature. This is also a state of living together with heaven and earth and being at one with all living things. In these circumstances, man is no longer isolated in a limited existence but is an entity that flows unobstructed in the outer world where he can experience the joy of the fish as it swims (*Floods of Autumn*) and converse with trees in his dreams (*The World of Man*). It is no longer just the standpoint of mankind: man can now understand the emotions of all living things and bridge the gulf between self and the opposite other to join the pulse of the universe.

This is neither a utilitarian state nor a moral state but a universal state of "alone in touch with the spirit of heaven and earth." (*Beneath Heaven*)

Fear of the beautiful

Mao Qiang and Li Ji were much admired beauties; on catching sight of them fish dived deep, birds flew high and the deer fled. (*Treatise upon the Ordering of Things*)

The ancient Greek philosopher Socrates, after much discussion of the nature of beauty, finally concluded that it was difficult. Reading this passage from Zhuangzi, the idea that "beauty is difficult" emerges rather easily.

Naturally, there is little similarity between the reasoning of Zhuangzi and Socrates on this point. Zhuangzi points out that there is a fundamental difference in the understanding of beauty between man and the animal kingdom comprised of the likes of fish, birds and deer. It is very difficult for the diverse world of living things to achieve a common standard, particularly over innate values such as ugliness and beauty and good and evil.

It is not only different species that differ in subjective judgement because of differences in their nature. Differences may occur in the same species due to era or epoch, tastes change with the times and there can be considerable divergences of direction. The Tang dynasty (618–907) favored a "soft smoothness of skin and a well-proportioned figure" as the standard of feminine beauty (Du Fu's poem *A Parade of Beauties*), or a tendency towards the ample. By the time of the Qing dynasty (1644–1911) one thousand years later, there was no way that Lin Daiyu, the very model of slender anxiety and heroine of the novel *Dream of the Red Chamber*, could be mentioned in the same breath as the imperial concubine Yang Guifei of the Tang dynasty.

On reflection, it may be that the reaction of the birds, fish and deer was not a question of whether or not they appreciated the looks of the two beauties but simply that they were frightened! To them a pair of beauties and a roughneck appeared exactly the same. Comparatively speaking, the choice between beauty and life as defined by Zhuangzi is obvious.

Dreams shed light on reality

In the past Zhuang Zhou dreamed that he was a butterfly, a fluttering butterfly, and was comfortable and happy as one. He did not know that he was Zhuang Zhou. Suddenly he woke and realized that he was Zhuang Zhou. He did not know whether Zhuang Zhou had dreamed that he was a butterfly or whether the butterfly had dreamed it was Zhuang Zhou. There must be a difference between Zhuang Zhou and the butterfly. This is called melding. (*Treatise upon the Ordering of Things*)

This is possibly one of the most beautiful dreams of vagueness and bewilderment in ancient China.

Dreams are mentioned a number of times in *Zhuangzi* but Zhuangzi himself figures in this one. Awaking suddenly, he remains deeply immersed in the *persona* of the fluttering butterfly, seemingly in disbelief and for a moment unable to distinguish between dream and reality, yet he is clear that there is definitely a boundary between these two worlds and that they can be separated. This demonstrates that at this point Zhuangzi is in reality. If he were still that happy little butterfly, busily enjoying itself, whence such clear knowledge of the distinction between the two worlds?

However, is this distinction absolute? Before the moment of "awaking suddenly" is the difference between Zhuangzi and the butterfly important? Isn't that feeling of happy content real? Do we really mean to say that this sort of feeling is illusory?

Dreams, in the real world, are difficult to grasp, but they are deeply connected to us. Through them we have a communication tunnel to a completely different world. This communication is real because we experience the joy of entering a different world and we sense that we can merge ourselves with all living things.

Zhuang Zhou and the butterfly, the intermingling of reality and dreamscape, certainly both perplexed and fascinated Zhuangzi. Since it was something that Zhuangzi had himself experienced and consequently the cause of countless daydreams, it was also the object of self-examination and involved the consideration of the true nature of the world.

Wake with a start and then sigh

Dream but not know that it is a dream. In a dream thinking that you are dreaming, wake and know then

that you were dreaming. (*Treatise upon the Ordering of Things***)**

As we sigh over life we often say that life is a dream.

Dreams are uncontrollable, we don't know when they will come or when they will go. They are vague and misty. Things that cannot happen in real life occur in dreams, whether joy or tragedy, yet within the dream our feelings are so realistic that we can be terrified out of our wits or shed tears of joy.

As we shiver in a cold sweat or weep with joy nobody knows that it is a dream. After an experience, either tragic or joyful, has passed its peak we may perhaps have a flash of the thought, "is this a dream?" However, this is only in passing and the dream continues. It is only when we eventually wake that we can finally confirm: "Yes, that was a dream."

This is the situation that Zhuangzi describes.

The relationship between dreams and reality excites us. People tend to ignore the doctrine of mutability that underlies the beautiful story of Zhuang Zhou dreaming that he was a butterfly in the *Treatise upon the Ordering of Things*. Instead, they become fixated upon the dim fantasy of whether it was the butterfly that dreamed it was Zhuang Zhou or Zhuang Zhou who dreamed that he was a butterfly. Once awake, there are actually very few dream situations where, as in the butterfly dream, reality and dream are intertwined. In the vast majority of dreams, the huge discrepancies between dream and reality are astonishing and frightening. The Tang dynasty poet Li Bai (701–762) once awoke from a dream sighing with regret because the fairyland he had just encountered had vanished in smoke before his eyes.

> My spirit suddenly shook
> And I woke with a sigh
> Alone with a pillow
> And without that twilight mist.
> The pleasures of the world
> Are the same
> And like all things past
> Flow down to the Eastern sea.

Poem of Remembrance of a Dream of Paradise

Another Tang poet, Li Shangyin (c. 818–c. 858), turned back from a marvelous dreamscape and wrote:

> Confused without a thread to grasp
> Light turns dark
> And ceaseless mist
> Breaks then joins.
> Awake I heard the rain upon the terrace
> And turned from the flickering lamp
> To sleep upon my pillowed hands.

A Dream After Listening to the Rain at Night with Graduates Wang and Zheng on the 28th Day of the 7th Lunar Month

Dreams and reality are still a part of life. Zhuangzi's final phrase suddenly elevates dreams to the realm of life and death: is the life of man then a dream or not? Conversely, is the so-called state of death then an awakening? To take it further, is life a short spiritual excursion and death a return to the *status quo*?

Know autumn at the fall of a single leaf

My life has a limit but knowledge does not. To pursue limitless knowledge with a limited life is both exhausting and perilous. (*The Essentials of Fostering Life*)

The fact that life has its limit is a limitation upon life. There are very many understandings on how a life of limits should be spent. Most people believe that riches and glory are important. In today's society people generally believe that study and knowledge are required to achieve them. This is not unreasonable.

The all-out pursuit of knowledge has been the spiritual direction of recent times. In ancient China at least, the pursuit of knowledge was not the be all and end all of life. The Confucians naturally regarded knowledge as important and Confucius was renowned for breadth of learning and literary ability; but the Confucians, in their pursuit of knowledge, regarded the nurturing of life as their basic objective and alongside "Sincerity and a Properly Aligned Mind," the "Investigation of Things and the Extension of Knowledge" were not to be overemphasized at the expense of other concepts. Daoist concepts strongly emphasized the view that an abundance of knowledge in no way represented wisdom.

Different tendencies have emerged from the space between limited life and limitless knowledge. Seen from the standpoint of life we should naturally grasp life. The single-minded pursuit of knowledge results, the further you go, in the acquisition of the systemics of knowledge but not of the wisdom of living. This wisdom has never been built on a basis of the accumulation of knowledge: we may sense autumn from the fall of a single leaf, we do not have to wait until every leaf on the tree has fallen before knowing that autumn has arrived.

Do neither good nor evil

Do no good to avoid fame, do no evil to avoid punishment. (*The Essentials of Fostering Life*)

These two propositions have aroused a great deal of discussion and controversy.

One school of criticism takes it for granted that good deeds do not seek fame; but for evil-doing to go unpunished, isn't that like telling people that crime should escape punishment? It just doesn't make sense.

In fact, the meaning should be understood in the context of the texts that precede and follow. The preceding text, also well known, "My life has a limit but knowledge does not. To pursue limitless knowledge with a limited life is both exhausting and perilous," already presents its analysis. Zhuangzi is not advocating the pursuit of knowledge at all costs, because he speaks from a standpoint based upon the life we live, and knowledge is not the home of life's core values. On the same principle, whether the deeds are good or evil, the fame or punishment that they bring about is entirely external, and although in the eyes of the populace at large there exists a distinction of good and evil between the two, they both harm the life of the self in the same way. Punishment goes without saying. As to reputation, people are always burdened by it: either good deeds once put in train cannot be ended and continue to the point of spiritual exhaustion, or the protection of one's good name vainly increases undesirable behavior, the person becoming hypocritical and betraying his original nature.

Consequently, speaking from the standpoint of the fundamental truth of life, "good" and "evil" both could be laid aside. Hence, the meaning of the two phrases is not to say that one may "do good" or "do evil" as long as one does not become entangled by fame or incur punishment, but is to say that one should not deliberately set about performing good deeds or doing evil. The final section of the *Webbed Toes* chapter puts it very clearly: "At top I dare not perform acts of benevolence, at bottom I dare not behave basely."

To do neither good nor evil is to adopt the "middle Way" (*zhong dao*). Standing behind this is the phrase, "Take the middle as your path." Guo Xiang, the Western Jin dynasty (265–316) philosopher and official, wrote in his commentary on Zhuangzi: "always follow the middle," leave behind virtue and evil and the good and bad of the secular world and take the middle path to maintain the integrity of life's original self, that is the fundamental meaning of Zhuangzi.

We can master emotions

If we can be content with the times and adapt to change, neither joy nor sadness can intrude. (*The Essentials of Fostering Life*)

In this quotation, the words "times" and "adapt" possess an underlying significance. This significance derives from the story of Qin Yi's condolences on the death of Lao Dan (another name for the late Warring States philosopher Laozi, the founder of the Daoist School).

After the death of Laozi, Qin Yi went to offer his condolences. He emerged after having only sobbed three times. Some thought this strange and asked him: "Were you not a friend of Laozi?" Qin Yi replied: "I was. I saw everybody crying bitterly, the old as if they had lost a child and the young as if they had lost a parent. I fear this is not what Lao Dan would have expected. As far as Lao Dan was concerned, he came into this world at the appropriate time and when the time came for him to leave, he adapted to the course of nature and left. If we are content with the times of coming and of going and adapt to the laws of nature, then the emotions of joy and sorrow cannot penetrate our hearts."

That is to say that in this context, the words "times" and "adapt" refer particularly to birth and death. Zhuangzi realized that the process of life incorporated irresistible limitations and that we had no control over arrival or departure. In a situation over which we have no control we can only understand and on the basis of that understanding calmly accept the limitations, taking joy in coming and feeling sadness at going. Since these emotional responses are of little help, we should not allow them deep into our inner mind to live there and cause harm. When there is no outward display of the emotions of pleasure or anger, it is largely for the benefit of the onlooker and has significance only in the eyes of others; when grief and joy do not enter the mind, that is truly a matter of the self and a protection of one's inner world.

First self then others

The complete man of ancient times realized himself first and others later. (*The World of Man*)

These days we generally feel that the order "others first, self later" is a good one. However, the ancients obviously did not.

This statement by Zhuangzi is a borrowing from Confucius who said that one should look after oneself first and others afterwards. He urged his disciple Yan Hui (521–490 BC) to curb his youthful enthusiasm and ideals and not to plunge wholeheartedly into travelling to the state of Wei and offering advice to its ruler on improving its disastrous government. He also suggested that Yan Hui was insufficiently aware of the saying that one should "accompany a ruler as you would accompany a tiger."

Perhaps you may think that in saying this Zhuangzi was merely acting as a mouthpiece for Confucius. However, Confucius had said: "Ancient scholars studied for themselves, those of today study for others" (*Xian Wen*). This is an expression of the same idea of "First Self then Others," with the importance of self given first place. The *Great Learning*, the first of the Four Books, a classic closely studied by innumerable scholars, enumerates the following ideas in order; the cultivation of self, the ordering of family, governance of the nation and peace under heaven. It starts with oneself, first achieve the perfection of self and then gradually ascend and expand through family and nation to the whole world. Although this ideal is on a grand scale, it envisages a basic route that is completely identical with the idea of "first realize oneself and then others."

That "self first," "the realization of self" and "self-cultivation" should precede "governance of the nation" and "peace under heaven" is not something that we nowadays find easy to believe in, and is considered selfish. Nevertheless, the belief that man should come first is most important of all. Achievement in any field first requires a concentration upon the self otherwise it would be like putting the cart before the horse and would lead to eventual failure. Confucius said very clearly: "Man may glorify the Way but the Way may not glorify man." (*Analects—Duke Ling of Wei*) In the final analysis, the promotion of the Way and the rise and fall of the world is down to man.

Listen closely with the mind

One should not hear with the ears but listen with the mind. (*The World of Man*)

The art of listening is one of the basic human virtues and demonstrates an ability to communicate as well as mutual understanding between people.

Animals are also able to communicate by making sounds, or through specific actions or even direct contact. They can co-ordinate group action, co-operate in hunting for food, and transmit warnings. Mankind can also perform these functions through speaking and listening. However, for mankind, the most important form of communication of all is not the reminding each other that it is time to eat or to go to work, but the achievement of mutual understanding.

This is an interaction between minds. Speech and listening do not stop at words, admittedly meaning and sense are to be found in phrases and sentences but they are also bound up with the externality beyond them. When parents tell their children: "Wrap up well, take care not to catch cold," this is the embodiment of an actual and real involvement and concern. This is not just something that the ears hear, it is something that has to be experienced.

Meaning is beyond speech: even more it is the fundamental means of expressing literature. For example, in poetry the words emanate from "here" the self, but the meaning resides "there" with the opposite other. The meaning that we express beyond speech, the overtones and implications, can only be heard in the mind.

Only birds in flight leave no trace

It is easy to disappear but difficult to walk without leaving a footprint. (*The World of Man*)

On the face of it, these two statements are both clear and easy to understand. If you want to leave no trace, then simply stay at home and don't go out, there will be no footprint. But if you insist on going out and still want to leave no trace, it will be difficult unless you can fly without touching the ground.

What does Zhuangzi mean? The Ming dynasty (1368–1644) monk Shi Deqing (1546–1623) explained in his *Commentary on the Inner Chapters of Zhuangzi* (*Zhuangzi Nei Pian Zhu*): "It is easy to escape from man and abandon the world, but it is difficult to be involved with the world without attachment and leave no trace." If you feel out of tune with the world, then just go and be a hermit, living in a purity where the eyes do not see and the body is not contaminated and where the dangers of deceit do not lie in wait for you. In fact, abandoning the world is a simple way of preserving oneself. On the other hand, to carry on living in the world and yet, like a bird crossing the heavens, to leave no track in the vastness of space, moving naturally and unhindered by any possible obstacle, that is truly difficult.

How is it possible, apart from emulating the flight just described, to reach this state? The answer is by following the ways of the world with a deep understanding of the principle of things and without attachment of self and letting external events take their natural course, rather

like the kitchen hand in *The Essentials of Fostering Life* who
butchered an ox using a blade "without thickness" to enter
the "with space" gaps of its skeleton so skillfully that the
blade suffered no damage in 19 years of use.

A roundabout way forward

**Act according to the urgings of man and it is easy to
become false; act according to the urgings of heaven
and it is difficult to be false. (*The World of Man*)**

Zhuangzi frequently emphasizes the difference between
"man" and "heaven." "Heaven" represents the laws of nature
and "man," as Zhuangzi saw him, embodied the particular
characteristics of the lack of harmony between "heaven" and
the world of man. Conduct motivated by human desire is
never in accord with the Way of heaven; it is "false," a word
used to describe human behavior that is not innate in origin.
Conversely, behavior that complies with the Way of heaven
is not false but genuine.

In order to adjust his relationships with others, the
man living in the mass of humanity has to abandon some
of his original needs for the sake of compromise; it is this
restraint and pragmatism that constitutes the "falsity" of
human behavior. You may be afraid of something, or you may
want something badly and consequently attempt to change
yourself in order to avoid it or to obtain it, to smile at faces
you dislike or force yourself to do things in which you have

absolutely no interest, taking a roundabout way of achieving your objective.

This was what Zhuangzi found tedious. He abhorred the tedium and so withdrew and lived according to his own natural preferences, believing in the truth of his own life and the sincerity of his own heart.

A negative character in *Zhuangzi* who moved later generations

At dawn I received the order, at dusk I drank iced water. (*The World of Man*)

She Zigao, a member of the royal family of the state of Chu, was once ordered by the king to undertake a mission to the state of Qi. This was a difficult task however, because the state of Qi generally showed great courtesy to foreign envoys but things always dragged on and She Zigao feared that he would be unable to accomplish his mission and would be punished by the King of Chu. Thus, although he normally ate and drank very simply, on this occasion he burned with anxiety and having received the order in the morning, in the evening he drank iced water to quench his burning thirst.

Zhuangzi considered that in general there was no need for a situation like this, one should maintain the peace of one's inner mind rather than be controlled by external events.

From looking down to looking up

Things are simple to start with but vexatiously complicated in the end. (*The World of Man*)

This quotation from Zhuangzi, based upon everyday observation and experience, speaks of a deep and common truth.

Judging from the original context of *The World of Man*, Zhuangzi was speaking in a negative sense. His perceptive observation of the ways of the world demonstrated to him that "those who succeed through the use of their wits start out upright and honest but always resort to shameful trickery in the end and in extreme cases could be described as outlandish. Those who drink wine out of politeness are courteous to start with but are befuddled later and in the extreme gain pleasure from loutish behavior. It is always the same, mutual confidence in the beginning ends in mutual trickery." Thus, Zhuangzi believed that things started very small and ended in major disaster. Faced with the situation that Zhuangzi describes, the correct strategy in response is to recognize the potential for minor events to develop into major disasters, to prevent their gradual spread and to take precautions in advance.

However, once shorn of its context it is possible to offer a positive explanation of this quotation: everything in the world, sentient or inanimate, follows a process of germination, development and maturity; the towering pavilion that starts on level ground, does it not begin from the ground up or even from an excavation, from looking down and then gradually needing to look up?

To beat is to care, to scold is to love

Good intentions can have ill consequences for the things you love. (*The World of Man*)

Zhuangzi tells the story of the stableman who spared nothing in the care of the horses he raised, even to the extent of using specially woven bamboo baskets and conch shells to remove their dung and urine. He once saw a horsefly biting the back of a horse and slapped it away. The horse did not understand his intentions and was suddenly angered, chewing through its bit and trampling the stableman underfoot. Zhuangzi described this as: "Good intentions can have ill consequences for the things you love."

Zhuangzi's point in telling this story was to illuminate the principle of the saying "accompany a ruler as you would a tiger." You may prepare counsel for a ruler and advise him with all your heart and with burning loyalty, perhaps bringing mortal disaster upon yourself. Zhuangzi's observation was acute. Consider how many loyal officials of the generations that followed Zhuangzi fell victim to disasters of life and family through provoking the ire of their ruler!

This might also serve as a hypothesis of a very considerable universality. One may be utterly devoted to another, even spoil them, and then something trivial can cause an outburst. Children who lack sense are often like this. Being in love is like it too; care too much for your partner and one is always more easily hurt.

Of course, love should find expression, concealing it is not an appropriate course of action. But love should not be excessive, excessive love leads to unbridled arrogance of behavior. The expression "to beat is to care, to scold is to love" if not interpreted literally can be regarded as a kind of solemn demand that we should turn our love towards the true interests of the person we love. In this sense it is acceptable.

What's the use of "useful"?

We fell the trees of the forest for their wood; we burn oil for lamplight. Cinnamon bark may be eaten and thus we fell the cassia; there is a use for lacquer and so we strip the bark of its tree. We all know the use of the useful but nobody knows the use of the useless. (*The World of Man*)

Zhuangzi was much given to the use of trees as an example when discussing the problems of life. This quotation refers to the usefulness of the lacquer tree. According to the *Records of the Historian*, Zhuangzi was once "an official of the Lacquer Garden," in one explanation the official in charge of an orchard of lacquer trees, so there may be some sense to this.

Forest trees are felled because in ordinary eyes they have a use; and it is precisely because of their usefulness that they sacrifice their lives. Trees that grow straight and tall are felled first, sweet well water is drunk first until it is exhausted (*Mountain Trees*), consequently Zhuangzi considers that the trees bring this disaster upon themselves. Much the same applies to lamp oil and lacquer trees.

Zhuangzi warns that we should not assume that the common definition of "useful" and "useless" will apply forever and that it should not be used as a standard against which to measure the value of everything. *The World of Man* records that when Nanbo Ziqi visited Shangqiu he saw an enormous tree, so huge that it could provide a canopy of shade for a thousand carriages. On closer inspection he saw that the branches were so twisted that they could not perform the important task of serving as roof beams and that the trunk was split so that it could not make an inner or outer coffin, tasting the leaves did injury to lips and tongue and the smell made you dizzy for three days. Nanbo Ziqi then regretfully concluded: "This tree is really no use and that's why it has grown so tall!" Similar trees that had achieved a long life through being of no use were observed when Zhuangzi led his disciples on mountain walks. Zhuangzi took the same view as Nanbo Ziqi: "This tree lived a long life by being useless." (*Mountain Trees*)

However, were these trees indeed as useless as commonly believed?

That depends in what sense they can be described as useful or useless. The trees may be described as useless in terms of utility but seen from the point of view of the preservation of life and achieving their natural life span, they are really useful! Conversely, the timber for beams may well be considered useful but its life has been extinguished and seen from the point of view of the trees themselves, what use are these uses?

Zhuangzi stands with life itself and proposes a conclusion that differs from the commonly held definition of useful and useless. There is a theoretical factor here that to a large extent has to do with the incessant mortal dangers of those times. The reality was cruel. There was a place called Jingshi in the state of Song where trees whose trunks grew to a size that could be encompassed by a single hand would be felled to build stockades for monkeys; those that grew to three or four handspans would be felled to provide beams; and those that grew to seven or eight handspans would be made into complete coffins. Truly not a trace of a survivor left!

Father and son and twins

Seen as a distinction, the distance between the liver and the gallbladder is as great as that between the states of Chu and Yue; seen as a similarity, all living things are the same. (*Symbols of Perfect Virtue*)

Zhuangzi was intensely self-aware of his perception of the paramount position of man. If you regard others from your own point of view then, naturally, you are right and the others are wrong, but what if you exchange points of view? Then the others may believe themselves right and that you are wrong.

This illustrates the fact that for many things in the world you have to consider the angle from which they are seen. The two phrases above are a case in point.

For example, even a pair of near identical twins will

display minute differences when consistently observed from the point of view of distinctions; but when a father and son are particularly observed from the point of view of similarity, people will then often remark: "Your son looks just like you!" However, we all know that even the most similar looking father and son cannot exceed the mutual resemblance of twins.

This hypothesis of Zhuangzi's not only appeals to the process of intellectual analysis but may also be of some emotional comfort. The Song dynasty (960–1279) writer Su Shi (1037–1101) was visiting the Red Cliffs by boat with friends when one of the guests lamented that the beauty of moonlight passed and life was short. Su Shi consoled him with words recreated from *Zhuangzi*: "Seen as change, then heaven and earth can never have existed even for a moment, seen as unchanging, then both self and things have no end" (Su Shi, *Rhapsody of the Red Cliff*). From the point of view of change, everything is changing, heaven and earth have never stopped changing for an instant, otherwise how could the blue sea change to fields of mulberry trees? Seen from the unchanging point of view, then there can be no end to us or all living things. Do we not all exist between heaven and earth?

Be still and one may comprehend the change in all things

Man is not mirrored in running water, he is mirrored in still water. (*Symbols of Perfect Virtue*)

Water is necessary to human civilization, not only does mankind derive the nutrients of life from water, water also provides spiritual inspiration. There is reason in Confucius' statement: "The wise delight in water and those with humanity love mountains" (*Analects—YongYe*). In the eyes of the Confucians, Zhuangzi and Laozi belonged with the wise and not amongst those with "humanity"; they looked on water with eyes of love.

Laozi derived his understanding of the universe from water. In Laozi's analysis the world was a system of complementary opposites in which "opposites are the motive force of the Way" and where all events and all things transmute into their opposites. For example, plants are tender as they grow but wither in the end. Consequently, Laozi proposes that by adopting a standpoint of weakness and adapting to changes in events and things one will naturally arrive at a position of strength. He sees water as the best symbol of this tendency: "Beneath heaven there is nothing weaker than water but there is no power or strength that can defeat it." (*Laozi*)

The drops of water that wear away stone, are they not like this?

Zhuangzi's attention is upon still, not running, water. He noted that it was only still water that would reflect an image and that running water gleamed and rippled in the light, there was motion in everything, nothing could be done. This was an everyday experience but one of profound significance: only a spirit as calm and unprejudiced as still water could comprehend all the circumstances of the world.

The mirror in literature, politics, and religion

There is no dust upon a bright mirror, if there was it would not be bright. Be much in the company of sages and there can be no fault. (*Symbols of Perfect Virtue*)

In both Chinese and Western culture, the mirror signifies clarity of reflection. In his novel *Red and Black*, Stendhal uses the mirror as a metaphor for the way literature should display reality, it should illuminate the deep blue of the sky but also reflect the muddy road. Mirror analogies were plentiful in pre-Qin China. Thus, Zhuangzi in his mirror analogies refers to dust, and says that if you want a clear mirror you should not allow it to become dusty, if it does it cannot reflect clearly. Mirror and dust metaphors are common in later intellectual traditions, for example, the Zen school used it as a metaphor for the importance of self-cultivation, the *Platform Sutra* records the *gatha* of the Sixth Patriarch Shenxiu:

> The body is a bodhi tree
> And the spirit the bright mirror and its stand,
> Polished and swept
> Clean of the dust of the world.

This *gatha* uses the mirror as a metaphor for the spirit and expresses the hope that it will be frequently swept clean of dusty contamination in order to maintain its purity.

There are many famous examples of the use of the bright reflection of the mirror as a metaphor for the illuminating qualities of the sages, perhaps derived from Zhuangzi. In his well-known admonition following the death of the Remonstrance Official Wei Zheng (580–643) the Tang emperor Taizong (598–649) said: "With bronze as a mirror one may adjust cap and robe, with the past as a mirror one may know rise and fall, with the sages as a mirror one may know the gains and losses of one's own behavior. I keep these three mirrors as protection against my own faults. With the passing of Wei Zheng, I have lost a mirror."

The beauty of the second eye

Where virtue grows, the fleshly form is forgotten. When man does not forget what should be forgotten and forgets what should not be forgotten, that is true forgetting. (*Symbols of Perfect Virtue*)

Man's appearance is heaven sent and generally speaking there can be no great possibility of change. However, inner self-cultivation may, to a considerable extent, be self-determined. When these two aspects are externalized one becomes beauty of countenance and the other beauty of temperament. Beauty of countenance is the beauty of the first eye and beauty of temperament becomes the beauty of the second eye. There is no doubt that on first impression beauty of countenance is overwhelming; everybody admires the concept of this particular "beauty." Gradually, however, the beauty of temperament imperceptibly reveals its fascination.

Zhuangzi records that Duke Ling of Wei was fond of

a man who stooped, had no lips and whose head and neck were covered in lumps. It would be impossible to say that this kind of appearance was lovable on first sight but one could certainly say that in all probability the initial reaction would be one of fear or even loathing. However, this man gradually gained the ruler's affection through the virtue of his inner nature. Here, "virtue" (*de*) means moral integrity. At the same time, it is a homophone of *de*—to gain—and refers to that inner part of man gained from the Way. The virtue gained from the Way should genuinely be assured and always kept in mind; by contrast, the externalities may simply be forgotten.

A prerequisite for the possession of the ability to appreciate the inner nature of ugliness and set aside externalities is real inner strength, this is the true growth of virtue. Otherwise, if you asked me to forget the external ugliness, what would there be to remember?

Do not concentrate on objects alone

Those who are deep in desire are shallow in innate understanding. (*The Greatest Teacher of All*)

Innate understanding is the natural ability to accord with the Way of heaven; it stands in fierce opposition to all lust and desire. The urges and pursuits triggered by desire can destroy the natural state of man's original nature and cause a loss of equilibrium. In truth, one's needs are limited, the thirst for acquisition far outstrips what can be received. Zhuangzi vividly pointed out: "The wren nests deep in the forest, it needs no more than a twig upon which to perch; the mole drinks at the stream, it needs its fill and no more." (*Wandering at Will*)

Once one's major spirit is wasted on these external pursuits, the very nourishing of life becomes problematical: this is what innate understanding refers to. Zhuangzi did not approve, either, of the pursuit of unlimited knowledge. The accumulation of knowledge does not necessarily lead to an increase in wisdom, consequently the image of the unkempt scholar reciting poems and ancient texts was not one that he appreciated (*The Essentials of Fostering Life*). In material terms, we have seen so-called collectors, their rooms awash with rarities and gleaming with pearls, yet with nowhere to set foot. This is man in the service of objects.

The Song dynasty polymath Su Shi loved paintings and calligraphy and always bought a few when he came across them but he thought little of it if they were carried off by others and did not regard it as a pity: "I may just as well enjoy the passing clouds or the song of birds" (*Record of the Hall of Precious Paintings*). He was very clear: "A gentleman may take an interest in objects but not pursue an excessive interest in them. Where he takes an interest, he may gain pleasure from an object though it may be small and not become obsessed though it may be precious; if he pursues the interest the small object becomes an obsession and the precious gives no pleasure."

All people have desires. If, like Su Shi, we do not pursue a deep interest in them then we cannot be submerged by them. This is called the possession of innate understanding.

Forget and return to the practice of the Way

When the spring dries up and fish are left together on dry land, they mingle their moist breath and keep each other damp; this is not as good as their state of mutual unawareness in rivers and lakes. (*The Greatest Teacher of All*)

Today the phrase "keeping each other damp" has a very definite positive sense. Zhuangzi would certainly not dissent from this view. He closely examines the actions and friendship of the fish in their dangerous predicament and describes it concisely and accurately. It is difficult to imagine any lack of a sense of compassion.

Nevertheless, Zhuangzi is capable of extraordinary feelings when in a situation away from ordinary people or perhaps when ordinary people hold to just a single point of view. This sense derives from his detachment from the passage of time. Zhuangzi bases his consideration upon the original state of all sentient beings. Fish should live in water, only in water can they swim freely; to be deprived of water is to be deprived of the natural state of life and that is a distortion of existence. Consequently, however much fish on dry land may support each other in their effort to survive, in the end their state is pitiable.

Back in the world of man, Zhuangzi, in his chapter

Master Knowledge Travels North, quotes *Chapter 38* of *Laozi*: "Lose the Way and there is virtue, lose virtue and there is humanity, lose humanity and there is righteousness, lose righteousness and there is propriety." In the ideological world represented by the Confucians, all this has an indubitably positive value but Laozi, Zhuangzi and the Daoists acutely pointed out that humanity and righteousness (*renyi*) was a secondary state that followed upon the loss of true Morality and that at a time when true Morality still existed there would be no necessity for humanity and righteousness in the same way that there was no necessity for the mutual concern of "keeping each other damp" when fish were in water.

If there is no necessity for the positive values of humanity and righteousness, then there can be no necessity for the distinction between right and wrong. Thus, Laozi said: "Rather than praise Yao and condemn Jie it would be better to forget them both and change their Way." Rather than judge between Yao the sage or Jie the despot, one should forget them both and return to the Way.

Returning to the Way is like a fish returning to water: "Fish forget each other in lakes and rivers, people forget each other in the practice of the Way."

Vote for Hundun

The emperor of the Southern Sea is called Shu, the emperor of the Northern Sea is called Hu and the

emperor of the Middle Sea is called Hundun. Shu and Hu often met each other on Hundun's territory and Hundun treated them well. Shu and Hu planned to repay Hundun's virtue and said: "Man has seven orifices, for sight, hearing, eating and breathing (*two eyes, two ears, one mouth, two nostrils*), only Hundun does not, we should try and drill some into him." They drilled for days and on the seventh day Hundun died. (*A Response to Emperors and Rulers*)

The story of Hundun exemplifies much of Zhuangzi's basic thought.

To start with, Hundun embodies in form an aspiration towards completeness, it is neither split nor fragmented, it is Zhuangzi's analogy for the primal state of the world.

Next, Shu and Hu mean "agile" and "quick" and hint at the passage of time; in the temporal dimension the world is ever changing, a question repeatedly considered by Zhuangzi and the early philosophers.

Next, with the passage of time the whole world split apart, a split which marked the end of the original state of the world and the death of Hundun's original nature.

Next again, Zhuangzi took an opposite view to the analytically critical approach to the world, whether in this case of the analysis of the actions of Shu and Hu in "drilling for seven days" or the knowledge-based spiritual activity of Hui Shi and Gongsun Long of the School of Logicians; on the contrary, he believed that one should be in communication with all sentient beings and directly face the diversity and color of all the sentient beings of the world.

Finally, Zhuangzi could not accept a view which took the one size fits all, "everybody has seven orifices" theory and, ignoring the individuality of every sentient being, attempted to impose its single aspect upon everybody. For example, Zhuangzi was critical of Hui Shi's view that the only standard of measurement for a gourd was the ability to hold water; why could one not use gourds that exceeded normal measurement to float on a river?

If we wanted to choose a figure that most closely represented the concepts of Zhuangzi I would very possibly vote for "Hundun." In the case of Laozi I would vote for "water."

Avoid confusion in major things

Minor confusion may lead to a loss of direction, major confusion may cause disorder of spirit. (*Webbed Toes*)

There is a kind of person who is confused in minor matters but sensible in major. They are confused the moment they step outside and lose their way; however, in major decisions, at the important crossroads of life, they prudently make the right choices.

As Zhuangzi described it, this sort of person belonged to the category of minor confusion and not to major. It was direction that was lost in minor confusion but in major confusion it is the fundamental, original nature itself. The bird that can find its way back to the nest does not suffer minor confusion but the bird that perishes through lack of food is in major trouble.

It requires a person of surpassing wisdom to avoid major trouble. The poet Tao Yuanming was one such. He started as a functionary and busily pursued an official career. In the end, he "lost his way a little but felt that the present was right but the past was not" (*A Ballad of Return*), realizing that he "lacked the heart for the mundane world when young and by nature thirsted after the rural life" (*Retiring to the Countryside*). By temperament he loved nature rather than the hubbub of official life and in an act of determination uprooted himself from official life and retired to the countryside where he found a place to settle down contentedly. He was the very antithesis of the victim of "major confusion."

This often occurs in the mundane world. The eminently successful man with no sense of that world, who perhaps really has a grip of his true nature and is without "major confusion" and who cleverly calculates every move and seems to proceed intelligently step by step, may perhaps, through a moment of confusion, take a road that runs in the opposite direction to his original true nature.

Is it right to give up life for a righteousness?

The common person sacrifices himself for gain; the scholar sacrifices himself for repute; the official sacrifices himself for his clan; the sage sacrifices himself

for all that is under heaven. Thus it is that that these people of different callings and of different repute are as one in their sacrifice of their own nature for the demands of the life of the body. (*Webbed Toes*)

Zhuangzi's greatest concern was the living of life. It was this that guarded the nature of self and allowed the years to pass calmly by without early death or vain attempts to live forever.

Nevertheless, as always, there are many temptations in life's journey and a multitude of duties to be performed and choices awaiting us. The concrete problem of why this happens is very often not the same in each case, moreover, what is a difficulty for some may be nothing at all for others. Take "gain" for example, something avidly sought by those with little, but a sage, by reason of his superiority to avarice, would not lose direction over a mere fly's worth of profit. However, everybody has their limits and when it comes to major difficulties in their own particular field they will, like the common person anxious for gain, make fatal choices.

Perhaps the sage who sacrifices his life for "all under heaven" has a clarity of self-awareness and his sacrifice is a consequence of his subjective choice, very different from the fatal involuntary pursuit of gain of the common person. Confucius said: "Scholars of will and those that possess humanity do not seek life at the expense of humanity but sacrifice themselves for the sake of humanity" (*Analects— Duke Ling of Wei*). Mengzi, when he said: "I desire life and I also desire Righteousness, if I cannot achieve both then I would sacrifice life for Righteousness," also expressed this same uncommon spirit. (*Mengzi—Gaozi Vol. I*)

However, Zhuangzi asks: Can this be right? No matter, for whatever reason, in the end it is life, the most precious thing in the world, that is lost. Thus, in terms of the "sacrifice of their own nature for the demands of the life of the body," are not the common man and the sage the same?

Whether you steal a lot or a little, it is all the same

All under heaven make sacrifices: those who make sacrifices for the sake of humanity and righteousness are called gentlemen; those who make sacrifices for goods and money are called common. Their act of sacrifice is as one, but the gentleman and the common man still remain. (*Webbed Toes*)

Since all "sacrifice their nature for the demands of the life of the body," the mistake is basically identical, then why draw distinctions between them?

The distinction between humanity and righteousness and goods and money derives from a worldly concept that seemingly pursues an aim where "this" is laudable and "the other" is despicable, that results in an even greater difference in reputation between the gentleman and the common man. In fact, is this really necessary? It is rather as if both having committed theft, it then becomes necessary to draw a distinction between one having stolen money and the other gold. How much significance can there be in this? Theft is the appropriation to oneself of things that do not belong to oneself. Perhaps there is a difference of value to the stolen objects, but can you argue that it is not theft because the things that this person has stolen are two hundred *yuan* less in value than those stolen by the other?

Zhuangzi gives the examples of Bo Yi and Dao Zhi. Bo Yi was a prince of the state of Guzhu who believed that the punitive expedition of King Wu of Zhou against the despot Shang Zhou was an act of rebellion and consequently attempted to obstruct King Wu's cavalry. He was unsuccessful and out of principle swore never again to eat the grain of Zhou and in the end died of starvation in the Shouyang mountains. By contrast, Dao Zhi (Robber Zhi) who: "At the head of 9,000 men laid waste all beneath heaven, seized cattle and horses and carried off wives and daughters" was a famous bandit who eventually died at Dongling (*Zhuangzi—Robber Zhi*). Between the two lies the difference between "gain" and righteousness but both died for something that they sought for themselves and both lost the basis of self.

If hell really existed, Bo Yi would probably not recognize Dao Zhi as a fellow believer, but I guess that Dao Zhi would regard Bo Yi as a comrade, since he too also spoke of "sagehood," "courage," "righteousness," "wisdom," and "humanity."

Collected achievements of the experience of a great robber

One of Robber Zhi's followers once asked him: "Does robbery too have a Way?" Zhi replied: "What is there that exists that does not have a Way? To sense the presence of treasure in a room, that is sagehood; to lead first, that is courage; to leave last, that is righteousness; to know whether or not to act, that is wisdom; to share the booty, that is humanity. There has never yet been a great robber who did not possess these five qualities." (*Pilfering Chests*)

Robbery has a Way? It talks of "sagehood," "courage," "righteousness," "wisdom," and "humanity"? This is an offence to society to be heard with a shudder!

But this actually is not very strange. The "Way" originally had many interpretations and each sage had his own.

Han Yu (768–824), the great Tang dynasty essayist and writer, wrote a major piece promoting the revival of Confucianism entitled *The Original Way*. It opened by saying, "Universal love is called humanity, and the appropriate practice of humanity is called righteousness and to follow both is known as the 'Way.' To be sufficient in oneself and not to wait upon the external is called virtue. Humanity and righteousness are established in meaning. The Way and virtue are unestablished in sense." Han Yu clearly points out that the "Way" refers to a path of implementation and that virtue is innate and requires no external additions. The two are "unoccupied positions" that can be filled with two different senses but the universal love aspect of humanity and the required rational behavior of righteousness both bear a particular meaning that reflects Confucian concepts.

Since the Way and virtue are "unoccupied positions" that can accommodate different values, why can they be used by Confucians and Daoists but not by robbers? The sagehood, courage, righteousness, wisdom, and humanity of which Robber Zhi speaks may seemingly use the vocabulary of Confucianism but they are closely bound up with the behavioral processes of thieves. Taking part in the first assault, allowing safety to others when withdrawing and keeping the danger to oneself, knowing whether matters will succeed or not, sharing the spoils equally, may be a summation of the experience of a "great robber." Zhuangzi's sharp wit is fully displayed here and at the same time it inspires us all to consider a problem: Does a generally positive value always have positive applications?

Bad people use good tricks

Without the Way of sagehood the virtuous cannot succeed, without the Way of sagehood the robber cannot practice. Thus, the advantages that sages bestow upon all under heaven are few and the damage they do is great. (*Pilfering Chests*)

Historically speaking there is, naturally, a positive aspect to the sage's theories about the governance of the world and the systems that were established as a consequence. However, these things were, as Laozi put it: "the sharp instruments of the nation," and since they were instruments, then everybody was in a position to use them.

We have already seen Robber Zhi using the values of sagehood, courage, righteousness, wisdom, and humanity, so revered of the Confucians, and how they became a comprehensive summation of the experience of the great robber. Does this not explain how, while the Way of the sages benefits the improvement of the lives of the people, at the same time robbers may also exploit it to achieve their own ends? In the eyes of Zhuangzi, "the Way of the sages" was merely an instrument, its positive or negative significance dependent upon the user. Many of the world's assumptions and systems are like this, they provide principles and safeguards for a course of conduct but the same conduct in different hands may absolutely acquire a different meaning: a broad thoroughfare (*dao*) may provide swift passage for a fire engine but it may also aid the escape of robbers.

Zhuangzi provided a lateral view of "the Way of the sages," that bad people could use good devices and that good devices could help bad people. Just think how much mental effort the robbers would have had to expend to refine their own experience without that set of Confucian values! Zhuangzi provides an example from daily life. To guard against pilfering, people often firmly lock or tightly rope chests and cupboards. This is quite right but when a great robber who makes a clean sweep of everything arrives, his only fear will be that nothing is either firmly locked or tightly roped. Because it was properly done originally it has even worse consequences in the end.

Zhuangzi further points out that because good people are in the minority and bad people in the majority, the chances of bad people exploiting "the Way of the sages" vastly exceed those of good people. Consequently, and taken as a whole, "the Way of the sages" does more harm than good in the world.

Zhuangzi's pessimistic view of mankind stands revealed as does his utter difference from the Confucians, for example from Mengzi, with his belief in "innate virtue."

The two hands of the great robber

The thief who steals a belt hook is executed, the thief who steals a nation becomes a prince, yet virtue dwells in the halls of princes. (*Pilfering Chests*)

The story of the thief who made off with everything was a warning to us of the existence of the distinction between petty thieves and great thieves.

The petty thief steals things like belt hooks but the great thief steals whole nations. This is not a fable from Zhuangzi but a harrowing history seen with his own eyes.

At the time, the state of Qi was a large country where villages stood side by side, birds and beasts called to each other, its population fished, farmed and weaved, and temples, gods and even its administrative organization existed in perfect order. However, lords of the Tian clan usurped the throne and within generations the original rulers of the Qi state had been completely replaced and though the clan's conduct resembled that of robbers they "enjoyed the stability of the mythical kings Yao and Shun, smaller states dared not offend and larger states dared not punish them." In this way the clan cleared out the state of Qi. Internally, the state appeared much as it had been, there was no perceptible disruption of life, society or government, the Tian clan had completely taken over the original political structure. Zhuangzi drew blood at the first blow when he observed that this was a complete theft of the state of Qi with its "rule of the wisdom of sages."

In this period, the "rule of the wisdom of the sages" became an effective tool of the usurpers and, as can be imagined, those who acquired the nations of others through theft continued to promote values such as loyalty and righteousness. Historically speaking, following a change of rule or dynasty the way new rulers accorded respect and even honor to those loyal to the previous dynasty who had so vigorously opposed them is a symptom of this. At this point, values such as loyalty cease to present any real danger and can become instruments for the protection of systems and their political legality, displaying another hand alongside the fist of naked violence.

This is the concept of "yet virtue dwells in the halls of princes." Power overcomes morality and morality shares its bed with power.

The best ruler of all is imperceptible

The ruler who is compelled to rule despite himself can do no better than rule through inaction. (*In Ease and Tolerance*)

To the mind of Zhuangzi, it was best not to assume the character of one who ruled from on high. In *Wandering at Will*, King Yao wishes to hand over to Xu You. The latter resolutely refuses saying: "You have ruled well, I have no need to abandon the sacrificial vessels to take over the kitchen." Zhuangzi himself politely declined the invitation of the King of Chu to become a minister, preferring to fish in a muddy pool instead. (*Floods of Autumn*)

What is to be done if one has no option but to engage in affairs? Inaction (*wu wei*) is the answer. But *wu wei* does not mean that one should abandon everything and do nothing. It means that one should move with the natural ebb and flow of the world, being neither forceful nor rash. Pulling up the roots to assist growth is both rash and forceful. Liu Zongyuan (773–819), the Tang dynasty essayist and poet, described how a hunchback named Guo was skilled in forestry. His particular skill lay in allowing the roots of the tree to spread naturally and the soil to be spread evenly. Once the tree was planted, he left it and no longer interfered with its natural growth, allowing its natural qualities to protect it (*Biography of Guo, the Hunchback Tree-Planter*): "Do not harm its growth," "If its nature is complete, its quality will succeed." These essentials of *wu wei* were well understood by Hunchback Guo.

The Daoists always advocated *wu wei* in politics and Laozi's Daodejing devotes considerable attention to it, for example, "the sage acts through inaction and instructs without words" (Chapter 2), "act without action and there will be nothing without governance" (Chapter 3), "can there be inaction through love of country and governance of the people?" (Chapter 10), "the sage proclaims inaction, the people enlighten themselves" (Chapter 57)—all these complement the formulations of Zhuangzi.

The supreme state of the political principles of *wu wei* is reached when the ruled are unaware of the existence of the ruler; where respect and admiration from above are already so prevalent below that fear of and contempt for the ruler has no basis for discussion. In his 17th chapter Laozi says: "It is best when those below are unaware of the ruler. Next best when they love and praise him. Next when they fear him. Next when they ridicule him."

Physical labor or mental effort?

Where there is machinery there is dexterity, where there is dexterity there is cunning. (*Heaven and Earth*)

A major milestone in the evolution of man has been his ability to manufacture and use tools; man no longer wrestles empty-handed with the world to combat external threats or deal with the difficult problems of life. Nevertheless, one of the figures in *Zhuangzi* opposes the use of new tools.

Zi Gong (BC 520–?) a disciple of Confucius, was once passing along the southern bank of the River Han when he observed an old man watering his vegetable patch. He had built a tunnel to a spring and was carrying water in an earthenware pot to water his vegetables, the effort was considerable but the results were meagre. Zi Gong suggested the use of an efficient hoist built from wood, light in front but heavy at the rear, which could raise water quickly. The old man listened and then not only did not thank Zi Gong but colored with anger and reproved him saying: "Using machinery requires dexterity, dexterity requires cunning; the possession of cunning means that the mind itself is no longer pure and simple, thus the spirit is troubled and how then can the Way be sustained? I am not ignorant of machinery but through shame I do not use it."

Superficially, the old man appears really opposed to machinery but what he says makes quite clear that his fundamental opposition is not to machinery as such but to the fact that the use of machinery produces a cunning that warps one's basic nature.

Consequently, Zhuangzi would rather weary the body than strain the mind.

Are tigers beautiful or not?

Simplicity, nothing beneath heaven can wrest its beauty away. (*The Way of Heaven*)

"Simplicity," a very ordinary word that at first sight may be understood as "plain and simple," is the most beautiful of all. It would be difficult to say that this explanation is wrong. However, it is not what Zhuangzi really meant. We might ask: That multiplicity of stripes on the tiger's body, is that beautiful? In fact, what we call simplicity should not be understood on the basis of the interpretation of plain and simple bestowed on it by aesthetic fashion.

One should go back to the original meaning of the two characters *pu* and *su* that go to form the word *pusu*: "simplicity." *Pu* (朴) meant wood that had not been worked and *su* (素) meant cloth that had not been dyed. The current phrase "presenting a plain (*su*) face to heaven" means a face without the application of make-up. When *pu* and *su* are put together to form a word the commonality between them produces the true intent of *pusu*, the maintenance of the original nature, unadorned and unaltered.

Zhuangzi presents a clear and vivid analogy of this layer of meaning in his *Heaven and Earth* chapter: a century-old tree had been felled, part of it went to provide the wood for the making of the ceremonial beakers, richly adorned in bands of gold, used in the rites of sacrifice; the remaining wood was tossed into a ditch. Seen from a worldly point of view, there may perhaps be the distinction between beautiful and ugly and superior and inferior, but in the loss of original nature there is absolutely no difference between the two at all.

It is clear that to Zhuangzi's mind it was not beauty that was supreme but the preservation of the purity of original nature: beauty was a consequence of the truth of original nature. Hence, the tiger's stripes were innate and Zhuangzi, with a nod, would have acknowledged their beauty and not insisted that they were ugly.

Do we need to go on learning?

What you study now, O Ruler, are but the dregs of the ancients! (*The Way of Heaven*)

Zhuangzi maintained an attitude of skepticism about the ability of words to express subtle or profound thought. In his *Floods of Autumn* chapter, he showed clearly the impotence of words and speech in the area of "the Way." Language was only effective in that part of real life that belonged to the "coarseness of things" and the "spirit of things" relied principally upon the imagination ("something that could be envisaged").

We can understand the "coarseness of things," it is an actual concrete object. But what about the "spirit of things"? Let us look at the following tale.

Once upon a time, the ruler Duke Huan was reading in a loud voice in his palace when a wheelwright called Bian put down his tools, approached the duke and asked: "What is Your Honor reading?"

The duke replied: "The works of the sages."

"Are the sages still alive?"

"No, they've passed on."

"Then what Your Honor is reading are the dregs of the

ancients!"

The duke was enraged: "I'm reading, how can you, a mere wheelwright, air your opinions? If you have reason, speak it, if you have not then it is a capital offence."

The wheelwright replied: "I speak from the occupation that I follow. If the mortices on the wheel rim are too loose for the spokes, the wheel will not be firm, if they are too tight the spokes will not fit, they need to be exactly right. My hands have such a sense, which my mind understands but I cannot express in words; there's a trick to doing it, a skill which I can't describe to my son and my son cannot receive from me. So, at the age of 70 I'm still working here as a wheelwright. The ancients have passed away, the things they couldn't pass on have gone with them. What Your Honor is reading are the dregs of the ancients."

When Bian was just talking about how a wheel should be, that still belonged to the "coarseness of things." However, when he discussed the skill or trick of making a wheel, which, although something that could not be conveyed in words, could be gradually understood through the practice of the hands and acquired by the mind, that was actually in the realm of the "spirit of things." Technology may be advanced but it is not a "Way," it still faces the world of "things."

Back to Duke Huan: Zhuangzi does not tell us whether the duke accepted the views of wheelwright Bian. Perhaps he abandoned books and followed the wheelwright in his craft. The ruler Wen Hui realized the nurture of life from his cook's butchering of an ox. Perhaps Duke Huan may have learned something as well?

If Xi Shi had not had a heart condition

Xi Shi had an illness of the heart and hence frowned. An ugly woman from her village saw her frown and thinking it beautiful returned to the village clutching her chest and frowning. The wealthy villagers seeing it closed their doors and did not venture out; the poor seeing it left with their wives and children. She knew the beauty of frowning but did not know why it was beautiful. (*The Movement of Heaven*)

When Zhuangzi says, "Simplicity, nothing beneath heaven can wrest its beauty away," the beauty lies in the preservation of the original natural state. From this, we can truly understand the significance of the story of the ugly woman Dong (East) Shi imitating a frown.

The reason that the frown of the imperial concubine Xi (West) Shi was considered beautiful was that it arose from her heart disease and was a manifestation of a real "heart" and not because she was a beauty and everything about her was therefore beautiful. The reason that Dong Shi's imitation of the frown was ugly was not because she was fundamentally ugly but because she had no sickness of the heart, so that her frown did not arise from her fundamental nature and was purely an act of imitation. Dong Shi's single-minded pursuit of the commonly accepted concept of beauty and her false affectation led to the loss of her true original self. One might imagine that if Xi Shi had not "frowned" because of "sickness of the heart," Zhuangzi might have laughed at beautiful women.

Zhuangzi constantly ridiculed the kind of behavior that defied the original self and blindly both accepted and pursued the mundane values of the ordinary world. We might also interpret the well-known story of "learning how to walk the Handan way," recorded in *Floods of Autumn*, from the same angle: A young man from the Shouling area of the state of Yan went to Handan in the state of Zhao in order to learn to walk the Handan way. In the end he failed to learn the new walk but also forgot how he had originally walked and was obliged to crawl home. Is this not also a loss of an inherent original result?

In fact, a "frown" is a mere mark, and imitating a frown was the external expression of Dong Shi's mistake. If one were to level criticism in Zhuangzi's terms then it ought to be *Dong Shi Xiao Xin*—Dong Shi imitating a heart.

Don't clothe the monkey

On water there is nothing better than a boat, on land there is nothing better than a carriage. A boat may proceed on water but seek to propel it on land and it will travel not a yard in a lifetime. (*The Movement of Heaven*)

It is to be feared that in reality no one can propel a boat on land or drive a carriage on water. Even if it were really the case, not travelling a yard would be a good result, at worst it would be like marching in the trail of a snail; a carriage on water would be death by drowning, perhaps only to be seen in films of flying car chases?

On inspection, this quotation broadly says that particular actions must conform to particular conditions and that violating the characteristics and limitations of external conditions and forcing an action can have no good result. Zhuangzi's intention was to demonstrate a difference from the outlook of the Confucian system. Confucius hoped that imitation of the Zhou dynasty, the last of the three first dynasties (Xia, Shang, Zhou) would restore the system of rites and music that had collapsed in his time. As Zhuangzi saw it however, the world of the past, even if it had been a golden era, was distantly separated from the present, as different as land and water, and that to impose the Zhou rites in Confucius' native state of Lu would lead to a result more or less like propelling a boat on land or driving a carriage on water ("Are not past and present as land and water? Are not Zhou and Lu as boat and carriage? To pray now to impose Zhou upon Lu is to push a boat upon land, a labor without success and disaster for oneself"). Zhuangzi pointed out that the laws of rites and propriety that governed the world should change and advance with the times. If you dressed a monkey in the robes of the ancient sage Duke Wen of Zhou, would the monkey be pleased? He would struggle for dear life, biting and tearing until he had thrown all off and was happy.

The logic of Zhuangzi's lively description of how the ancient system of rites could not be applied to the current world is clearly elucidated; but it is interesting to note that seen from here Zhuangzi also acknowledged that Duke Wen of Zhou's system of Rites was not too bad.

Leisure is the cradle of thought

To labor in body without rest brings fatigue, to consume the spirit without cease is toil, and toil exhausts. (*The Constraint of Will*)

The Daoists placed considerable importance on the maintenance of life. At the fundamental level life may be divided into two aspects, physical and spiritual; in neither should there be excessive toil.

Zhuangzi vividly recounts a tale about the physical aspect in his *Attaining Life* chapter. Dong Yeji was a skilled charioteer who had an encounter with Duke Zhuang of Lu. The line of chariot and horse as he advanced and withdrew was perfectly straight and his turns were perfect, like a circle drawn by a pair of compasses. The Duke was amazed and believed him the best ever in the world, asking him to execute a few more turns. Yan He, a courtier, watched and then said to Duke Zhuang: "Dong Yeji's horse is going to fail!" The duke did not think so but said nothing; sure enough, in a little while, the horse faltered and the duke asked Yan He how he knew. Yan He replied that the horse was already tired in spirit and exhausted in body when more was demanded of it, naturally it failed.

This is also true of the spiritual aspect. The West has a saying that leisure is the cradle of thought. In China, Liu Xie (c. 465–532) of the Southern Qi and Liang period of the Southern dynasties (479–557) wrote ancient China's most systematic work of literary criticism, in which he emphasized the need to avoid exhaustion in the

spiritual act of literary creation by proceeding in a state
of leisurely relaxation ("relaxed in nature and harmonious
in interaction"). Historically, although there was a school
of "bitter and laborious recitation" (*kuyin*) poets, it seems
to have been a counter-example where the constant
expenditure of considerable spiritual energy produced little
in the way of results. For example, the Tang dynasty poet Jia
Dao (779–843) wrote of his lines:

> Walking alone, reflected in a pool,
> I take my rest against a tree.

that:

> Three years for two lines
> And my eyes flowed with tears
> At a single reading.

In the end, the poets of "bitter and laborious recitation"
were hardly mainstream.

In modern society, the protection of both body and
mind still remains an important problem that is now even
more pronounced. The more toil there is, the more one
should relax. Has not "leisure" already caught people's
serious attention?

Pure joy is rooted in one's nature

In the past, ambition was not for the achievement of
carriages and crowns but for the attainment of joy
without excess. Today's ambition is for carriages and

crowns but they are not part of one's heaven-given nature. The sudden arrival of mere objects is fortuitous. (*The Repair of Innate Nature*)

Li Bai said in a poem: "Life's achievement lies in joy to its limit" (*An Invitation to Wine*). Perhaps Li Bai's "life's achievement" may have been the deployment of a lifetime's political ambition, or a flight to the Daoist fairyland. Li Bai's joy was not without cause, though the cause, in Zhuangzi's eyes, was perhaps not truly worthy of joy: Zhangzi did not believe in worldly success, nor did he think eternal life was natural.

Zhuangzi believed that the power and status so important to man came by chance and left by chance. A passage in the *Tian Zifang* chapter contains the tale of Sun Shu'ao who was asked by Jian Wu: "Why, when you held the office of prime minister three times and lost it three times, was there no display of joy, anger, grief or grievance?" He replied: "I could not refuse when it came nor hold on when it departed. Loss and gain are not self-determined, thus there is no sorrow. What is there outstanding about me?" Status and power are not integral to one's original nature, they come by chance and lodge with us for the moment.

Zhuangzi was devoted to a true, pure joy, rooted in life itself and in man's original nature. It is the ability to preserve the originality or "originalness" of life that is most worth joy. This kind of joy does not increase because of popularly acknowledged external values and is what Zhuangzi acknowledged as an "ambition."

Fashionable colors from Paris

Those who sacrifice self to the material and lose their nature in worldliness are known as people who are upside down. (*The Repair of Innate Nature*)

"Material" (*wu*) stands in opposition to "self" (*ji*) and "worldly" (*su*) in opposition to "true" (*zhen*); loss of the self and loss of the fundamental truth is to be upside down.

The inability to maintain equilibrium between the external material world and self in the blind pursuit of external things, and the inability to look back and examine oneself thereby coming to value self, are two states very common to both past and present. "Man dies for riches, birds die for food," both of these are a kind of externality. Think for a moment, where is the purpose in acquiring riches and food? Isn't it in existing and living a little more comfortably? However, to actually forfeit purpose to the pursuit of means and to lose one's life in the process, who then would be left to enjoy the riches and food?

The pivotal influence of worldly concepts is strong already, particularly in today's society where the development and circulation of information has allowed the general circulation of ideas to far outstrip the past. In the past, a considerable amount of time was required before a concept achieved large-scale circulation. Nowadays it resembles "duckweed shivering at a breath of wind," swiftly "raging at the mouth of mountain caves" (Song Yu, *Fantasy on Wind*). The effect can also be considerable: a butterfly flutters in Brazil and there's a storm in New York.

How many people can be spared the influence of worldly concepts? Moreover, how many of these widely circulating "things" are really in the interest of your own nature? For example, the fashionable colors from Paris, how far do they agree with the physique and complexion and even the aesthetic direction of Asian people?

The problem does not lie in differences and distinctions; the unprecedented wealth of the modern world provides an opportunity for the appreciation of differences. The problem is "Seeing difference then thinking of change," having seen something then, heedless of one's own situation, to pursue it out of admiration to the detriment of one's own fundamental truth.

There can be too much education

One cannot speak of the sea to the frog in a well, it is confined to a void; one cannot speak of ice to the summer insect, it is trapped in time; one cannot speak of the Way to the person of prejudice, he is tied by education. (*Floods of Autumn*)

This quotation describes what the sea god Beihairuo explained to the arrogant river god He Bo in the *Floods of Autumn* chapter. On analysis it reaches a single conclusion on the basis of two analogies. The first two phrases are analogical and the final is the conclusion. The well in which the frog lives is the restricted space of its life; hence the phrase "frog at the bottom of a well," an analogy for self-satisfaction and narrowness of knowledge and experience. In the phrase "one cannot speak of ice to the summer insect, it is trapped in time," it is the dimension of time that is given prominence. The two phrases completely cover the dimensions of time and space and clearly demonstrate that the basis of the reasoning behind the phrase "little knowledge is not better than great knowledge" in *Wandering at Will* lies in its existential background.

The two relative phrases in "one cannot speak of the Way to the person of prejudice, he is tied by education" cover an overall analogy. The person of prejudice is biased and of little knowledge and experience. Zhuangzi mentions such people a number of times; in the *Way of Heaven* chapter, where "rhetorician" becomes "person of prejudice," and in the *Beneath Heaven* chapter, where those who are "neither complete nor universal" are also "prejudiced functionaries," their inability to understand the Way deriving from the limitations of their intellectual training; a rather subtle way of putting it. In terms of normal understanding, knowledge is a positive but in the eyes of the Daoists knowledge may simultaneously affirm some things while actually denying other things, at the same time both bestowing and depriving: knowledge is in itself a kind of gash in the integrity of the universe.

The *Beneath Heaven* chapter contains a warning: "In distinguishing the beauty of heaven and earth, in separating out the principle of living things and dissecting the techniques of the ancients there are few who can accord with the pure beauty of heaven and earth." To impose

meaning and order upon all the various things of the
world in order to construct a system is a basic intellectual
characteristic and also a precise explanation of the processes
of separation and analysis described in the chapter.

Is this warning simply an anti-intellectual concept? I
fear that one cannot put it that way. Zhuangzi warns us to be
aware of the limitations of knowledge and while illuminating
one corner to realize that perhaps blindness may exist in
other respects, particularly when one stubbornly clings
to one's own research. Cultural characteristics stand even
more powerfully in opposition to intellect and education;
no culture can be applicable everywhere. *Wandering at Will*
tells of the man from the state of Song who travelled to the
south to sell hats in the land of Yue. However, the people
of Yue wore their hair short and went naked and tattooed,
and to them clothing was entirely superfluous. The people
of Song were descendants of the Shang dynasty and to them
the ceremonial headwear of the Shang was an indisputable
symbol of civilization but attempting to market it in Yue
was, it has to be said, to be trapped in the confines of one's
own cultural cognition.

A chat with Zhuangzi

**Coarse and fine apply to the measurement of that which
has form; that which is formless may not be measured;
that which cannot be encompassed cannot be counted.
That which may be spoken of in words is of things**

coarse; that which may be sensed through perception is of things fine; that which cannot be spoken of in words or sensed through perception cannot be considered in terms of either coarse or fine. (*Floods of Autumn*)

Historically speaking, it has always been considered that Zhuangzi harbored a considerable suspicion of language, a view that "language cannot fulfil meaning."

Generally speaking, this is not a bad interpretation. But in absolute terms there are problems. It is legitimate to ask: If all speech is truly unable to express subjective meaning, then how does Zhuangzi communicate? Wouldn't this be a waste of words?

In fact, Zhuangzi's consideration of the problem is rather more subtle. His analysis of the things of the world (*shiwu*) divides them into two categories, those "with form" and those "without form." The formless cannot be grasped in minute detail: some are so small that they can be split no further; some are so great that they cannot be encompassed. Put simply, these formless existences cannot be grasped or described in language. With the "formed," Zhuangzi takes a step further and divides them again, into "coarse" and "fine." Zhuangzi clearly states that the "coarse" "may be spoken of in words"; the "fine" are difficult to convey precisely in words but may be grasped through the exercise of thought. The terms "coarse" and "fine" are of no significance to the existence of the "without form" category, "without form" transcends the terms coarse and fine.

Then what is it that the terms "with form" and "without form" actually indicate? There is a phrase in the *Zeyang* chapter that could well be used as an explanation: "When words are exhausted and awareness is at its utmost, that is the furthest extent of *wu* (things)." Thus, language and intelligence are limited to understanding and grasping the concept of *wu*, they cannot go beyond that. In Zhuangzi's conceptual world, the Way and things (*wu*) are regarded as relative opposites. In the *Floods of Autumn* chapter, they stand in opposition: "The Way has neither beginning nor end, *wu* has life and death." *Wu* is all the phenomena of our world, it has life and it has death, but the Way is perpetual and transcends both life and death. At this point we come to realize that Zhuangzi's fundamental standpoint is the belief that even though language may bring order to the phenomena of the material world and can be grasped and transmitted, it is powerless when it comes to the Way.

Thus, if we had the good fortune to meet Zhuangzi, we would at least be able to discuss the concrete world of reality, to chat about the weather for example, but it would be better to keep off the Way.

Standing on the great Way

Perceived from the Way, there is neither noble nor base to the material world; seen from the material world, self is noble and the other is base. (*Floods of Autumn*)

In the thought of Zhuangzi, there is a great gulf between the "Way" and the "material world" (*wu*). They belong to different spheres.

The Way is complete and transcends the individualistic material world, consequently it is not fixated on distinctions such as those between noble and base, hence the phrase "there is neither noble nor base to the material world." As for the material world itself, its individualism and egocentricity have given rise to various categories of distinction such as base and noble, large and small, becoming major symbols of the establishment of the concept of self. In particular, everyday situations affirm the greater value and status conferred upon "self" while at the same time denigrating the relatively low value judgement attributed to "other," hence "self is noble and the other is base."

Both historically and in reality this kind of situation is very common. For example, during the period of the Disputes of a Hundred Schools there was the view that "when the Way is different there can be no discussion" (*Analects—Duke Ling of Wei*). During the Western Han dynasty, the historian Sima Qian used the quotation above in a *critique* of the dispute between Confucians and Daoists: "Those who study Laozi condemn those who study Confucius, those who study Confucius condemn those who study Laozi saying 'when the Way is different there can be no discussion,' can this really be the case?" From this one can imagine the state of mind of those caught up in the vortex of a dispute while today, however, the topic of enthusiastic discussion is the complementary nature of Confucianism and Daoism in the Chinese cultural tradition and their joint construction of the spiritual traditions of Chinese culture.

In this we stand with the "Way."

Limits upon the utility of the things of the material world

Roof beams may be used as battering rams but they cannot stop a hole, and we say these are different functions; the wonder horses Qiji and Hualiu could gallop a thousand *li* in a day but were not as good as a weasel at catching rats, and we say these are different abilities; owls can catch fleas and see the tip of a hair at night but cannot see a mountain in daylight, and we say these are different natures. (*Floods of Autumn*)

There is a multitude of difference and distinction between the things of the material world and although Zhuangzi stood with the Way, he believed that all these various things had a reason for existence and were fundamentally equal; however, he was not blind to the reality before him and accepted the outward appearance of the differences between things.

Differences between things may be seen and touched but what is important is that they should be equally regarded in our minds. Here, "equally" means that they should all be regarded as part of the heavenly construct, free from the imposition of a structure of high/low, good/bad based upon an individualistic and biased view that seeks to take "this" (self) and dismiss "that" (other). There is a phrase in *Floods of Autumn*: "East and West stand in mutual opposition, but they cannot be without each other." East and West are naturally opposite each other and distinct, the sun rises in the east and sets towards the west, it cannot be the other way round. But although they work in different directions, they are mutually interdependent. Were there no east then there would be no west.

Since we should regard them equally, it is only reasonable that everything should exercise its possibilities to the utmost according to its nature. Beams have their long and their short, the crux lies in how you use them. In *Wandering at Will* Huizi says that the gourds he has grown are too big and thus cannot be used to ladle water; Zhuangzi comments that you clearly don't understand the uses of something large ("clumsy to use large")! He suggested that large gourds could be tied about the body and their buoyancy used to float in rivers and lakes. Stick to one's own view and large gourds are useless, follow the innate nature of things and there is considerable use.

All the sentient beings of the world differ in nature but when their nature is followed, all will exercise their possibilities to the utmost. This is where Zhuangzi stands in facing the multitude of things.

Observing the Way and moving with the times

Those that know the Way are bound to understand reason (*li*), those that understand reason are bound to comprehend the concept of moving with the times (*quanbian*), those that comprehend this will not allow external things to harm self. (*Floods of Autumn*)

Nowadays we conflate the two characters *dao* and *li* into

daoli (道理)—basis or justification. In fact, in ancient times there was still some distinction between the two: *dao* (the Way) was at a much higher level and *li* (reason) was a little less applicable. For example, it was possible to speak of "the Way of heaven" (*tiandao*) in the same breath as the "principle of things" (*wuli*) but very difficult to do so in reverse: "the principle of heaven" (*tianli*), the "Way of things" (*wudao*). Once this distinction is understood the first phrase becomes clear: understand the greater *daoli*—basis or justification—and the concrete reason will also be understood. What the phrase describes is a sense of an all-encompassing strategic view, unstoppable, like water pouring from the roof gullies of a tall building.

The phrase that follows describes how people who understand the principle of things can respect all sorts of conditions and find the means to adapt to circumstances. It should be noted that moving with the times and events (*quanbian*) is not unprincipled behavior akin to the grass on the wall top bending with the prevailing wind, but a judgement of time and trends premised upon the comprehension of the "Way" and of "reason" (*li*), a higher state that combines flexibility with principle. Confucius displayed some of this thinking when he said in the *Zihan* chapter of the *Analects* that one might study together but not necessarily seek the Way, one might seek the Way together but not necessarily behave with propriety, one might behave with propriety but not necessarily respond to events and move with the times. From this one can see that *quanbian* is an extremely elevated state, difficult to grasp and hence, in terms of sequence, a practice in which mastery comes slowly.

The final phrase means that if you comprehend how to move with the times and events you will naturally not be harmed by external factors; if at the same time as protecting self you know how to skirt danger, then you will not come face to face with irresistible pressure and sacrifice self in vain.

If you took an example from Confucius, would it not be Ning Wuzi who displayed extraordinary stupidity when faced with national disorder? (*Analects—Gongye Chang*: "When the state is without the Way then there is stupidity.")

Between heaven and earth—the man of nature

Do not use man to destroy heaven, do not use intent to destroy inherent nature, do not sacrifice virtue to reputation. (*Floods of Autumn*)

The key phrase of these three should be, "Do not use man to destroy heaven." It is an overall concept.

The Confucian philosopher Xunzi (c. 310–237 BC) sharply criticized the classical sages in his *Explanations of Error* and said of Zhuangzi: "Blinded by heaven and ignorant of reality." Leaving aside, for the moment, the question of whether Xunzi's criticism is correct or not, there is some strength to his observation that the crux of Zhuangzi lay in an emphasis upon "heaven." Heaven and man stand in opposition and the core concept of Zhuangzi was the goal of conforming to heaven. Taking only similar formulations into account there is this in the Inner Chapter of *The Greatest Teacher of All*: "Do not use the mind to add to the Way; do not use man to assist heaven, this is called a true man." "Do not use the mind to add to the Way" means not using man's knowledge to abandon the Way; "Do not use man to assist heaven" means not using the achievements of man to add to the natural law. This is clearly the meaning of "Do not use man to destroy heaven"—that is if we understand "destroy" in its broader sense of injury or damage rather than in its narrower sense of eradicate.

The phrase "do not use intent to destroy inherent nature" is similar in structure to those above where "innate nature" and "intent" between them constitute a relationship of relative opposites similar to that between "heaven" and "man." Nature is one's original nature or life, "intent" implies a certain craftiness. Ridding oneself of intent and following nature is to abandon cunning and comply with the will and Way of heaven. "Do not use intent to destroy inherent nature" speaks even more of maintaining man's inherent nature in the mundane world and rendering it invulnerable to distortion.

"Do not sacrifice virtue to reputation." "Reputation" in this context represents everything of the mundane world. It means not losing one's own virtue on account of all the various "things" of the world. This applies in particular to maintaining the integrity of self against the values and interests of society.

In sum, these three phrases require us to be a natural person who is in accord with the Way of heaven.

Preserving life at all costs in times of trouble

Zhuangzi was fishing in the River Pu. The ruler of Chu dispatched two envoys to say: "I would burden you with office over all within the borders!" Zhuangzi gripped his rod and paid no attention saying: "I hear that in Chu there is a turtle, dead already for 3,000 years. The ruler has it wrapped in cloth in a box and stored in a temple hall. Would this turtle rather value being dead leaving its bones behind or alive and dragging its tail in the mud?" The two envoys replied: "Alive and dragging its tail in the mud." "Away with you! I will drag my tail in the mud," said Zhuangzi. (*Floods of Autumn*)

This tale is perhaps the most well-known incident of Zhuangzi's life. The historian Sima Qian described a similar event in the biography of Zhuangzi he included in his *Records of the Historian*.

Why was it really that Zhuangzi refused office?

Zhuangzi's presentation of the opposing stories of the much-revered dead turtle and the living turtle with its tail in the mud, in order to induce the two envoys to make a choice, reveals that his basic consideration was the fundamental position of life. "Dragging one's tail in the mud" may appear a vulgar activity but it is in reality the natural state of a turtle's life; the "sacred turtle" in the temple may have been an object of veneration but that state was not predestined by the turtle itself, rather it was something bestowed upon it by mankind and moreover premised upon a loss of life. The inability to live life as it should be and the inability to preserve one's own life both violated Zhuangzi's basic beliefs and may be the justification for his refusal of office.

Another level is the experience of reality. Zhuangzi regarded the times in which he lived as a world of chaos, and bitterly considered that "in the world today one can barely escape execution"(*The World of Man*). He had probably seen too many examples of turbulent official careers ending fatally over the problem of power. There is a story in *Lie Yukou* (the Daoist philosopher known as Liezi) chapter that could well be taken as evidence. There was a man who had received a reward of ten chariots from the ruler of the state of Song to whom Zhuangzi related the following tale: a son retrieved a valuable hoard of jewels from an abyss, his father urged him to smash the jewels to smithereens at once; the black dragon that guarded the hoard was dozing and once it woke all hell would break loose! The ruler of Song is also taking a nap, said Zhuangzi; if he wakes you will be torn to pieces and your bones ground to powder!

Zhuge Liang, the late Han dynasty military strategist, remarked in his *Scheme for the Dispatch of Armies* that: "If you wish to survive in troubled times, do not seek fame amongst princes." This could serve as an explanation of Zhuangzi's thinking.

Gazing after the homing goose

Huizi was minister of the state of Wei and Zhuangzi went to visit him. Someone said to Huizi: "Zhuangzi is coming and wants your job." Huizi was frightened and searched the country for three days and three nights. When Zhuangzi saw him, he said: "In the south there is a bird like a phoenix called a Yuanchu, do you know of it? It flew from the Southern Ocean to the Northern Sea. It would only perch on the wutong tree, eat bamboo shoots and drink sweet water. However, an owl who had found the rotting corpse of a dead rat looked up as the Yuanchu passed overhead and said, 'Shoo!' to frighten it away. Are you now trying to frighten me away with your country of Wei?" (*Floods of Autumn*)

When Su Shi was living in exile in Huangzhou he wrote a poem (*Busuanzi—in the metre of The Fortune Teller*) with the final lines:

> Like a bird accustomed to the icy twig
> I cannot perch at ease
> But would rather dwell
> In the lonely cold of a sandbank.

In the depths of one of life's valleys Su Shi was still unwilling, even disdainful of associating with the common world. As for the soaring Yuanchu bird, it goes without saying.

Positions of power and influence in society are much sought after by ordinary people, this is easy to understand; once attained, trouble is taken and effort expended to maintain them, that too is understandable. However, we also need to understand that this is not the ultimate state of being. Like the owl, who presents such an image of defeated misery, it ought to be asked what is life really for?

Is it to worry about loss and gain on account of all these externalities? Perhaps in your single-minded devotion to the upkeep of all this, you may be losing the possibility and the joy of soaring away into the distance.

Life is not just about the maintenance of immediate advantage. We must know how to let go, to look up at the Yuanchu as it flies past and to gaze after the homing goose and follow it as it disappears into the distance, imagining what kind of scenery might be there.

All sentient beings are interconnected

Zhuangzi and Hui Shi were strolling over a bridge across a canal. Zhuangzi remarked: "Fish swim in a leisurely way, that is the pleasure of fish." Hui Shi replied: "You are not a fish, how do you know a fish's pleasure?" Zhuangzi said: "You are not me, how do you know that I don't know the pleasure of fish?" Hui Shi replied: "I am not you and thus do not know you; you are not a fish and thus cannot know a fish's pleasure and that's all." Zhuangzi said: "Be so good as to stick to the fundamentals. In saying 'how do you know a fish's pleasure,' you already knew that I knew and hence were asking me whence I knew. I knew from the bridge."
(*Floods of Autumn*)

Over the years, Zhuangzi's discussion with Hui Shi on the bridge has become entwined with people's minds.

Hui Shi was Zhuangzi's most important debating colleague and possessed clarity of logical analysis. At the level of reality he considered that Zhuangzi could not know whether fish were happy or not. Although it is said that there are people who understand the language of birds, for example, Gongye Chang, the son-in-law of Confucius, in reality nobody seems to have come across them. Nevertheless, Zhuangzi was quite definite that the fish were happy. A rigorous analysis of the language of Zhuangzi's response to Hui Shi certainly indicates that it is logically problematical.

Hui Shi's question was: You are not a fish how then can you know the pleasure of fish? Zhuangzi then cunningly adjusts the sense of "how" to mean "whence, where from," hence his answer, "I knew from the bridge." We cannot say that Zhuangzi's argument is logically consistent, what is more apparent, however, is his quickness of wit.

Nevertheless, is Zhuangzi wrong?

The world is not just realistic and it is not just logical. What Zhuangzi displays is a spirit that understands heaven, earth, and nature and is in unimpeded communication with all the sentient beings of the world. The fish is swimming in the water, I am on the bridge. The same easy command of sense and feeling, self and fish merged as one. The pleasure of the fish is actually a projection of my pleasure; I am pleased, therefore the fish should be pleased. These lines from *Sights of Spring*, a poem of the Tang dynasty poet Du Fu (712–770) describe the poet's reaction to scenes of desolation and destruction at Chang'an in spring in troubled times;

In defeat my very feelings
Weep as I see the flowers open
And my mind despairs.
Fear grips my heart
And I tremble
At the call of birds.

Perhaps this poem may be called in evidence to display the grief of destruction in the material world while Zhuangzi's tale of the fish expresses his own inner joy; first grief then joy.

Zhuangzi held to his own impressions; it is the detailed factual analysis of Hui Shi that stands in opposition. There are times when this world of ours cannot be explained through analysis; human feelings cannot and ought not be analyzed, once under analysis feeling no longer exists, for example, once lovers start to analyze and argue, separation is not far off.

Using reason to change feeling

Zhuangzi's wife died. Hui Shi called to offer his condolences and found Zhuangzi squatting with legs wide apart, drumming upon an earthenware vessel and singing. Hui Shi said: "You lived your life with her and raised sons, she died of age: would not failing to weep have been enough? But to drum and sing, is not that taking it too far and adding insult to injury?" Zhuangzi said: "It is not so, how could I not have felt sorrow when

she died? But after giving it careful thought, I find that in the beginning there was no life; not only was there no life, even form did not exist; not only did form not exist, even breath was lacking. Change occurred in a moment of vague confusion and produced energy, energy changed to form, and form changed to produce life. Now she has changed again and died. It is the same as the cycle of the four seasons, spring, summer, autumn and winter. She lay asleep in the chamber of the heavens and I followed weeping loudly. I believe that this was because I did not comprehend the nature of life sufficiently and that is why I no longer weep in grief." (*The Utmost Joy*)

The common saying goes, "Man lives by a single breath."

This is very straightforward, but the information that it reveals is very important. In ancient China the question of life and "energy" (*qi*—breath/energy/vitality) was a major topic. In *Master Knowledge Travels North* Zhuangzi clearly says, "Life in man is the concentration of *qi*. Once concentrated there is life, when dispersed that is death." This explanation of life and death through *qi* rather resembles the concept of cause and effect combining to produce sentient life found in Buddhist teaching. Zhuangzi's drumming and singing at the death of his wife is, in logic, the use of the concentration and dispersal of *qi* to interpret life and death.

Zhuangzi's recollection of his wife as a history of arrival and return indicates that originally there was neither existence nor form; that then gradually, in vague confusion, *qi* assembled, acquired form and life and that it now had returned to its original state. This journey of arrival and departure, like the succession of spring, summer, autumn and winter, creates a cycle: the "life" of mankind. Elsewhere, Zhuangzi refers to the change from life to death as being basically predestined: "Life and death are a matter of fate; as constant as day and night and ordained by nature." (*The Greatest Teacher of All*)

Having thought through this point, Zhuangzi was freed from his initial grief and wept no longer.

This conclusion conforms to Zhuangzi's fundamental concepts. Zhuangzi regarded all the sentient beings of the world as parts of a whole and although life and death were, in ordinary eyes, totally different, from an overall perspective they were all connected in a state of mutual succession. The chapter *The Greatest Teacher of All* contains the story of four friends, Masters Si, Yu, Li and Lai, whose friendship was based upon their unanimity of view on life and death. If someone could take the head of a lifeless form, use the section in which life existed as the backbone and use death as its tail section, if someone could understand that life and death, existence and destruction belonged to a single continuous form, then we could be friends with them.

Believing that life and death were the concentration and dispersal of *qi* and further that they could be understood as part of the beginning and end of a continuous cyclical process enabled Zhuangzi to neutralize his grief. This process not only had significant implications for changes in Zhuangzi's own life, it had an especial significance for the whole of China's cultural history: Zhuangzi proclaimed that although we cannot and perhaps should not cast off the emotional injuries of life and death, we can understand them and use reason to change feeling and overcome grief.

Some people live, but are dead already

The maintenance of form must be preceded by matter but there are instances where matter is more than sufficient but form is not maintained. For there to be life there can be no departure from form, but there are instances where there is no departure from form but life has already left. (*Attaining Life*)

In the first place, life is a material existence. The basic conditions for the maintenance of life are of course artefacts such as food and shelter, thus, "The maintenance of form must be preceded by matter." However, a life of high living, luxury and indulgence is not guaranteed to be the best state for the maintenance of life; excess is as bad as insufficiency, obesity and unmentionable diseases are frequently the lot of modern man, thus, "there are instances where matter is more than sufficient but form is not maintained."

To Zhuangzi's mind, of course life was important but it did not in any way merely equate with the material existence of form. In his chapter *The Constraint of Will* he criticized several kinds of people including those who practiced breathing, jettisoning the old for the new, imitating the actions of bears and birds in exercising their limbs, training breath and body, seeking to live a long life like Peng Zu.

Zhuangzi's concept of life was to live his allotted span in accordance with nature. Thus, though early death in mid-course was of course not a good thing, futile attempts to extend life beyond its limits were also inappropriate. In this sense, the mere maintenance of corporeal existence could not be described as a continuation of life as before; spiritual but not physical death would resemble a walking corpse. This is one of the levels of meaning in the phrase "instances where there is no departure from form but life has already left." To take it a little further, perhaps one could say that in "maintenance of life" what is to be maintained is the true life force where "life" possesses an internal value; if life force and value have been lost then "life" has long gone, thus: "Some people live, but are dead already." (Zang Kejia, 1905–2004, poem *Some People*)

Ignorance is bliss

A drunkard falls from a carriage and although injured does not die. His bones and sinews are the same as other men but his injuries are not, because his spirit is entire. He was unaware of riding in the carriage or of falling from it. He harbored no anxiety over life and death, this is why he collided with the material world without fear. (*Attaining Life*)

This is an exceptionally interesting tale and one perhaps based on actual experience. The odds on a drunkard suffering injury as opposed to somebody sober are much lower. The clear-minded person in danger is always frightened and as the common saying puts it, frightens himself to death; the drunkard, however, with his mind in a state of confusion, "harboring no anxiety over life and death," is unembarrassed by danger and walks treacherous terrain as if it were a level plain.

This is clearly a function of the mind; if the mind believes it dangerous then dangerous it is, if the mind believes it safe then safe it is.

As to "ignorance is bliss," people often draw negative conclusions and because of lack of a sense of danger or difficulty dare where others dare not. Naturally there are plenty of opportunities for failure but also for success. There will never be a time for success in failure to dare.

The common language of Confucius and Mengzi

Confucius was visiting the state of Chu and saw a hunchback catching cicadas with the sticky tip of a pole just as if he were picking them up. Confucius asked: "Is there method (*dao*) to your skill?" "There is," he replied, "If after long months of practice I can balance two balls on a pole without them falling off, there is no great loss; if I can balance three, I lose only one in ten cicadas; if I can balance five, then I can easily pick them up. My body is bent and cannot move, like a tree stump; the reach of my arms is like the shriveled branches of a dead tree. For all the extent of heaven and earth and the number of sentient beings I know only the catching of cicadas. I concentrate my mind, I neither sway nor tip, no sentient being can replace my concentration upon the wings of a cicada, how can I not catch them!" Confucius turned and said to his disciples, "See! No dissipation of will, hence the concentration of spirit and it is an old hunchback of whom I'm speaking!" (*Attaining Life*)

Mengzi was of the same generation as Confucius, however, there seems to have been no interchange between them and neither ever mentioned the other. Nevertheless, they still shared the same language, for example, both were advocates of mental concentration.

In the main, Mengzi directed himself to the question of study and in his *Gaozi* recorded the tale of the famous chess player Qiu teaching chess. One pupil concentrated only upon listening to Qiu explaining chess and the other, although he listened, paid no attention and thought only of how he might shoot a passing goose with his bow as it flew by. The difference in standard of the two may be imagined.

What Zhuangzi provides here is a story of catching cicadas. The old hunchback balancing three or five balls on the tip of a pole really seems like acrobatic juggling and there's the sticky catching of cicadas as well. But how does this superb skill become possible? The old man's experience was to concentrate his mind solely upon cicadas to the

exclusion of the brilliance of the outside world and not to
exchange his attention on the cicadas for anything else.

Put simply, the crucial link in achievement on earth
is single-minded concentration and the need to avoid
dissipating attention.

When the stakes increase

**Gamblers who bet with tiles are clever, those who bet
with belt hooks are cautious and those who bet with
gold are out of their mind. Their skill may be the same
but once engrossed with the game the externalities gain
in weight. All those who give weight to what is without
become dull within. (*Attaining Life*)**

There is no great difference between the ability to balance
required in walking along a line on the ground or walking
along a tightrope in the air. On the ground or in the air
it is still your frame of mind that matters: the inability to
walk along a line on the ground merely causes a sigh of
exasperation; falling from a tightrope may leave you half
dead, so naturally there is a difference in feeling. However,
it is precisely this difference in feeling that most easily leads
to mistakes. The experienced tightrope walker gathers
himself together, concentrates his mind and utterly excludes
external influences. The principle of Zhuangzi's remarks
about gambling is the same; as the bets increase in value, so
the mental pressure and strain becomes greater and greater

and the original sense of gay abandon turns to fear and even mental confusion and loss of judgement.

People's skills and sense are the same but if they care in particular for outcomes that are real they may not be sufficiently exercised. Isn't this a universal state of affairs? We have often met people who can move others in a heart-to-heart talk but faced with a crowded audience in a large hall can barely utter a word because, in fact, they are truly concerned about the way they express themselves.

"All those who give weight to what is without become dull within": the inner minds of people who are engrossed with externalities will sink and atrophy. At the head of the first chapter of his poem *Eugene Onegin*, Pushkin quotes his contemporary Prince Vyazemsky's poem, *First Snow*: "And it hurries to live and hastens to feel" (tr. Mitchell—"it" being youthful ardor). Perhaps one should pause in one's haste, return to the inner mind and listen carefully to the sound of one's heart to recover clarity of mind.

The cleverness of stupidity

Caught between the useful and the useless. (*Mountain Trees*)

Generally, this phrase conveys a hint of irresponsibility.

However, in this case it is a conclusion born of Zhuangzi's own experience. The story told in *Mountain Trees* goes like this: Zhuangzi was once walking in the mountains with his disciples and came across a large tree with flourishing leaves and branches; a woodcutter stood beside it but had made no move to cut it down. Zhuangzi asked why and he replied: "It's useless." Once off the mountain Zhuangzi stayed with an old friend who was delighted to see him and told the boy servant to kill a goose in his honor. The boy asked: "One goose can call, the other can't, which one shall I kill?" "The one that can't," said the old friend.

Sometimes uselessness may secure long life and sometimes it may cause death. Faced with this dilemma, Zhuangzi could only reach the conclusion that he did.

How to exist intelligently in dangerous times is a major problem. It may be that stupidity, or more accurately assumed stupidity, is the proper expression of intelligence in this situation. Confucius once said of Ning Wuzi of the state of Wei that when the state was both principled and enlightened he was wise; when it was unprincipled and in darkness he was stupid. His wisdom was to be acquired through study but his stupidity was not to be acquired. (*Analects—Gongye Chang*)

Ning Wuzi seems truly to have been a fine example of somebody "caught between the useful and the useless."

The solitary sail reflects the limits of the sky

As you cross a river and float on the sea, you look for the far shore but cannot see it, the further you go the more you do not know where the very end lies. When those seeing you off turn back from the shore, that is

when you are far away! (*Mountain Trees*)

There are many passages in *Zhuangzi* that are rich in feeling and seem to serve as models of literary expression for later generations. In this case, the section "As you cross a river and float on the sea" originally referred to shedding involvement and transcending the mundane world but the general understanding that it described a scene of parting would not be out of place.

A few brief phrases encompass both the traveler and those who see him off. For the distant traveler the road ahead is without end and the far shore is invisible, the further he travels the less he knows where he will end; those seeing him off watch the traveler from a distance as he gradually disappears into a final parting and then one by one turn back from the shore. The final phrase, "that is when you are far away!" envelops both parties in the feeling of a traveler floating away into the far distance.

Because of the Way, the practitioners of Daoism in *Zhuangzi* travel in profundity day after day, their companions of the Way naturally become fewer and fewer and their days more solitary. The scattering of those who see them off is an analogy for this.

A standard of measurement for troubled times

Those who combine for the sake of advantage abandon each other in times of disaster; those who combine out

of natural affiliation care for each other in times of disaster. (*Mountain Trees*)

In his exposition of principle Zhuangzi is never direct but tells you a story instead. Having never acquired his exceptional mastery of imaginative construction, I will provide an actual example.

What is "combining for the sake of advantage"?

Lian Po, the famous pre-Qin general of the state of Zhao, had a large entourage of hangers-on who abandoned him when he lost office; the moment he was reinstated they reappeared like a swarm of bees. Lian Po was enraged by this band of lickspittles who responded to his anger by saying: "All under heaven operates according to the laws of the market, when you have power we follow you, when you do not we leave, that's the principle of it, what have you to grumble about?" (*Records of the Historian—Biographies of Lian Po and Lin Xiangru*)

This tale not only tells us what "combining for the sake of advantage" is, it also tells us that those who come together for the sake of advantage will always disperse for the sake of advantage.

"Natural affiliation" refers to relationships born of a natural inclination. In the face of difficulties and misfortune those whose relationships are conducted along these lines will always stick together and support each other. We have all heard the metaphor; the family is the harbor of warmth and safety.

Nevertheless, there are exceptions.

During the period of the Warring States, Su Qin

(d. 284 BC) the exceptionally rich and successful statesman who became prime minister of the Six States, was unsuccessful in his youth. Having left home to promote his political ideals he returned empty handed and dispirited. Confronted with the ashen-faced Su Qin, his wife kept to herself and continued weaving, his sister-in-law refused to cook for him and his parents ignored him. (*Strategies of the Warring States—Qin*) Su Qin thereupon devoted himself to his books. If he got tired, he pricked himself in the thigh with an awl to keep himself awake and studying. When later he became famous and successful, he returned to his ancestral village once more. His parents travelled 30 *li* to meet him, his wife's attitude turned to one of immense respect and his sister-in-law crawled before him in obeisance. He asked her why she had displayed arrogance then and respect now, to which she replied: "You are now both rich and powerful." Su Qin sighed regretfully and remarked, "Without money and power your parents do not consider you their son, but once rich and successful your relatives respect you, behold the importance of wealth and power in this world!"

One of the standards of measurement for troubled times is whether natural affiliation can percolate through the way of the market.

Coming together and dispersing without cause

The social intercourse of the gentleman is as mild as

water, the social intercourse of the rogue is as sweet as wine. (*Mountain Trees*)

In ancient China "gentleman" and "rogue" were two social categories that stood in mutual opposition to each other.

Gentlemen recognized each other instantly by virtue of similarities of character, interests and environment, a so-called "smile at a glance without intervention of mind" (*The Greatest Teacher of All*). Their relationship, built upon common convictions and the foundation of mutual appreciation that derived from them, required no excessive external expression because of its intrinsic congeniality. Perhaps there may have been no contact for some time but in their innermost being they recognized each other and like the steady flow of water over time, on meeting again there was no impediment to continuing as before.

In stark contrast to the quiet waters of the gentleman running deep is the warmth of the relationship between rogues, as strong as sweet wine and as thick as thieves. Lives that lack true beauty hanker after the sweet taste of joy; by contrast those who have really tasted beauty understand the true sense of the ordinary.

The true gentleman can distinguish the contrast between gentleman and rogue. In the *Wei Zheng* chapter of the *Analects*, Confucius remarks, "The gentleman is sociable but does not collude, the rogue colludes but is not sociable." The collusion of rogues is association for the purposes of conspiracy. Since between rogues there is no true congeniality of spirit, no moral consensus or practice, the end result is always a falling out and division.

Zhuangzi added a further phrase to the two quoted above: "Without cause to join together there can be no cause to part." This is a startling use of "cause." Rogues come together without reason and disperse without reason; this is the great difference from the friendship of the relationship between gentlemen.

Be used to wrong and it becomes right

Become accustomed to muddy water and one loses the source of pure spring water. (*Mountain Trees*)

Very often, when emerging from darkness into light you can't help but screw up your eyes. Not because there is something wrong with the light but because you have spent too long in the dark and have lost the sense of normal perception. To always be immersed in muddy water almost obliterates any sense of fresh spring water. This is a metaphor for the loss of one's original nature, of seeing the strange as not strange and becoming so used to wrong that it becomes right. At this point one can understand the real strength of the following lines of the poet Gu Cheng (1956–1993):

> Darkness gave me eyes of black,
> But I use them to seek the light.

The heart of man is more dangerous than mountain torrents

The gentlemen of the central states understand propriety and righteousness but are hopeless when it comes to the human heart. (*Tian Zifang*)

This is Zhuangzi's criticism of Confucius. The Confucians advocate propriety and righteousness, however, in Zhuangzi's eyes these are not qualities integral to human nature but external rules established through the process of building society; for the Confucians to regard these externalities as basic is to hold the human heart and human nature in contempt.

How then does Zhuangzi perceive human nature? In the traditional interpretation, human nature is the relatively stable component and the heart represents the active component. By contrast, in Zhuangzi's concept of human nature, it is the aspect of original human nature that stands out. He considers it basically neutral or indifferent; furthermore, his profound examination of the lively and active human heart was enough to demonstrate that he was qualified to describe the Confucians as "hopeless when it comes to the human heart."

Interestingly enough, Zhuangzi once borrowed the voice of Confucius to propose that the human heart was difficult to understand. It was steeper and more winding than a mountain torrent, more difficult to understand than the workings of the heavens; the purposes of heaven were difficult to know but there was still the procession of the four seasons and the alternation of day and night. However, the inner being of man was deeply concealed. Some people appeared open and honest without but were arrogant within, some appeared frenetic but were actually quite reasonable and some appeared strong but were inwardly weak and so on (*LieYukou*). Moreover, once the heart leaped into action, it was even worse. Suddenly up then down, suddenly cold then hot, soft then hard, one moment calm as the depths then tumultuous as the heavens, the human heart was the most exciting and difficult to control (*In Ease and Tolerance*).

Zhuangzi was possibly the earliest philosopher to sufficiently recognize the extreme importance of the need for tranquility of the inner being.

Death of the mind and mind with the purity of dead ashes

There is no greater sorrow than the death of the mind, it exceeds death of the body. (*Tian Zifang*)

This is a topic that people today are happy to talk about.

Physical death is obviously a tragedy but it is a natural inevitability and Zhuangzi proposes we should accept it with equanimity and as it comes. Moreover, although Zhuangzi valued human life, to his mind the maintenance of physical health was secondary. "Mind" however, represents the human spirit, and when that dies, even if the body continues to exist, it is no more than a walking corpse.

The death of the mind means that someone loses the

certainty and consciousness of self, loses interest in living and means they have abandoned life on earth and that nothing can exist, nor can it ever.

It is worth mentioning that the "death of the mind" referred to here is not at all the same as the state of "mind with the purity of dead ashes" frequently mentioned by Zhuangzi in *Treatise upon the Ordering of Things* and elsewhere. This latter is an extreme description of a state in which all desires and superfluous knowledge have been jettisoned to the point of achieving an utter void of tranquility where your inner being is not moribund but is preparing to accept the arrival of the great Way. In Zhuangzi's chapter *The Greatest Teacher of All*, Confucius discusses "seated meditation" with Yan Hui. Seated meditation is a means of abandoning physical form, doing away with intelligence and then becoming as one with the great Way.

The phrase "mind with the purity of dead ashes" is not followed by nothingness but by a miracle and the hope of communicating with an even greater heaven, earth, and universe.

> In our depths we are ready to receive
> Those unimaginable marvels.
>
> Feng Zhi (1905–1993), *Sonnet I*

Listen and observe in humility

Heaven and earth possess a great beauty that is not spoken of, the four seasons possess a definite law that

is not discussed and all sentient beings possess original principles that are not mentioned. (*Master Knowledge Travels North***)**

Zhuangzi always treated interminable chatter with suspicion. What he really liked was a direct interface with the world and the universe, and to live and prosper in common with all sentient beings, not to regard them as objects for description and analysis. "Not speaking," "not discussing" and "not mentioning" is the sense of the quotation above.

The ancient philosophers, as they looked upon the world and all sentient beings, were well able to understand their majesty, beauty and natural order. However, they were unlike later generations when the spirit of man had become self-centered, lacked reverence and only harbored a utilitarian sense that took it upon itself to presume that "not speaking," "not discussing" and "not mentioning" meant "cannot speak," "cannot discuss" and "cannot mention." These later generations even considered that the outside world simply had no life and that they could rule as they pleased. Confucius once lamented, "Must the heavens need speak? Yet the four seasons proceed ..." (*Analects—Yang Huo*) There is no difference between this idea and the quotation from Zhuangzi above.

To learn the news of the universe, we need to listen to the voice of nature with humility.

A model for the *Orchid Pavilion Preface*

Woods and hills, rivers and plains cause me both delight and joy! But even when joy is yet unfinished, sorrow succeeds it. I can neither resist the coming of joy and sorrow nor prevent their departure. What grief it is that people are just a temporary lodging place for things and for feelings. (*Master Knowledge Travels North*)

Zhuangzi emphasized the naturalness of the human character, the need for man to become one with heaven and to expunge the actions of intellect and desire from men of all kinds. In the first passage of *Treatise upon the Ordering of Things*, Zhuangzi describes how Nanguo Ziqi, the Minister of War under the 7th century BC king Zhuang of Chu, "seated with the appearance of seasoned wood upon a bench and with a mind of the purity of white ash," represented the state of becoming one with heaven. As a result, Huizi posed the question: "Is man then without feeling?" (*Symbols of Perfect Virtue*) Some people even asked whether Zhuangzi wished to turn everyone to stone.

Despite the complexity of the problem, we can first establish that although Zhuangzi was excessively critical of emotion, he was, in fact, a deeply passionate man, with real feelings and capable of understanding feeling in others. If you doubt this, consider the following passage which reflects the sense of the quotation:

"In the natural surroundings of forests and rivers, a mood of pleasure and joy arises of itself, however joy and sorrow are interlinked and one follows the other, the arrival of joy and sorrow are irresistible and man becomes their host." This is a clear demonstration of the fact that in Zhuangzi's eyes, the occurrence of feelings was a natural process as well.

Amid this, we may be clear about how joy occurs but there is no simile for the "why" of the existence of sorrow. One can, perhaps, consult the *Orchid Pavilion Preface*. During the Eastern Jin dynasty (317–420), the calligrapher Wang Xizhi (321–379) held a gathering of friends at the Orchid Pavilion on Mount Kuaiji in Shaoxing, in present day Zhejiang Province, where they drank wine and composed poetry. The poetry was edited into a collection with a preface that became known as the *Orchid Pavilion Preface* and because of its calligraphy, "the first collection of cursive script under heaven." In the *Preface*, the scholars described how they assembled "in great joy" beneath "clear skies in clement weather, under towering mountains and precipitous crags, in luxuriant forests and flourishing bamboo." However, the *Preface* went on to say that joy could change in the instant and in the end, considered at a deeper level, everything passes and disappears without trace, so that one sighs, "how could this not be painful?" The process of joy turning to sorrow described in the *Preface* is identical with *Zhuangzi* and one could say that this passage from *Master Knowledge Travels North* is a model for the *Orchid Pavilion Preface*. However, the latter clarifies the source of sorrow more explicitly; in saying "life and death are the great question" the *Preface* quotes from Zhuangzi's chapter *Symbols of Perfect Virtue*. This too is a question that Zhuangzi had repeatedly and deeply considered.

Zhuangzi was thus profoundly emotional and therefore sought a road to emotional understanding and a road to the resolution of the suffering that arises from feelings.

Keep silent about that which cannot be spoken of

To cease knowing at the unknowable, that is knowledge! (*Gengsang Chu*)

The Daoists were dubious about the unlimited quest for knowledge. On the one hand, it was not the same as the acquisition of wisdom about life and on the other hand, knowledge was limitless.

The students of the early Greek philosopher Socrates once asked him: "Master, your knowledge is several times greater than ours and your answers to questions are always correct, so why do you always doubt your own answers?" Socrates drew two circles, one large, one small, and answered: "The area within the large circle represents what I know and the area within the small circle represents what you know; everything outside the two circles represents the unknown. Naturally my knowledge is greater than yours but the circumference of the large circle is greater than that of the small circle and the extent of the unknown with which I am in contact is naturally broader than yours. This is the reason why I often doubt myself."

In this kind of difficulty, Zhuangzi's response was not to extend the area of his knowledge, that is, to make the size of the circles even larger; that way, the unknown that faced him would naturally increase. He chose to stop, admitting that it was part of the territory of heaven he could never occupy. He believed that true knowledge lay in stopping at the border between the point where you could halt and the point where you could step no further.

The modern philosopher Wittgenstein (1889–1951) once said: "what we cannot talk about we must pass over in silence …" Zhuangzi would have nodded in agreement.

How the virtuous should conduct themselves

Those who face the world with an air of virtue win no hearts; those who through virtue place themselves below others cannot but win hearts. (*Xu Wugui*)

People of sagacity possess intellect and ability beyond the norm. They transcend the ordinary, but in the end they exist in society, so that how they should live alongside others and how in these circumstances they should fulfil their obligations and realize their sagacity requires some thought.

Guan Zhong (c. 723–645 BC) was a well-known politician of the period of the Warring States who, through the strong recommendation of the minister Bao Shuya, gained a position under Duke Huan of Qi, assisting him to achieve hegemony through the "nine alliances of the vassal princes." When beyond hope and at the point of death Duke Huan asked him: "If you were at your last gasp, to whom would you entrust the state of Qi?" Duke Huan had set his heart on Bao Shuya but Guan Zhong expressed the view that he would not do: "Bao Shuya is a man of unsullied reputation who does not seek the company of those who are not like him, moreover once he hears ill of someone he never forgets. If he were to rule the state, high and low would not get on and in the end they would offend you." Duke Huan continued to ask after a suitable choice and Guan Zhong suggested Xi Peng, great-grandson of Duke Zhuang of Qi, for his ability to build relationships with superiors and inferiors; his superiors felt that he scarcely existed and his inferiors would not betray him, while he himself was ashamed that he lacked the sagacity of the Yellow Emperor and yet at the same time had sympathy enough for those unlike himself. Guan Zhong continued: "Those who face the world with an air of virtue, win no hearts; those who through virtue place themselves below others cannot but win hearts."

Guan Zhong's loyalties were to the nation, his ability to set aside intimates and benefactors like Bao Shuya who had helped him in the past may have earned him respect; of greater rational value, however, were the criteria that he left for the observation of exceptionally able and gifted people: that those in positions of eminence and power should abandon status, should adopt an attitude of humility and respect and tolerate and feel sympathy for those beneath them.

Between with and without

One must know the useless before discussing what is useful. The world is neither narrow nor limited, what man uses is space enough for a footprint, when you dig alongside and reach the springs of hell does that space still have any use? (*External Things*)

Zhuangzi repeatedly responded to the problem of the so-called "useful" and "useless." In *Wandering at Will* he took issue with Hui Shi's theory of the uselessness of the large gourd, pointing out that Hui Shi's mind was stuffed with rubbish and insufficiently agile: Why not use a large gourd as a device for floating in a river or lake rather than stubbornly sticking to a fixed rule that gourds were just for holding water? It can be seen that in considering what is useful and what is useless, there arises the question of approach, using something one way may be useless, but a change of method may perhaps make it much more useful.

At this point Zhuangzi produces a different and rather clever argument: "The wren nests deep in the forest, but only on a single twig." (*Wandering at Will*) You can only occupy a very small piece of ground, does that mean you can get rid of a place barely big enough for your two feet? Of course not! What Zhuangzi is saying is that useful and useless are relative opposites. If you only want to keep the useful and get rid of the useless, then in the end the useful will be useless.

Laozi's view on the relationship between "with" and "without" somewhat resembles Zhuangzi's line of thinking:

"A vessel of clay is useful only for its emptiness. When the window spaces are cut only then can a room be used as a house." (*Chapter XI*) In manufacturing a vessel, one cannot just concentrate upon its form; a vessel becomes useful by virtue of the part that contains emptiness. The same applies to the logic of windows; a window frame naturally possesses both shape and use but the most important part of a window is the part that opens and closes, this is where light and air are accepted.

The reality of the world lies in this kind of presence and absence.

You must cross the bridge in the end

Traps are set for fish, catch the fish and forget the trap; nets are set for rabbits, catch the rabbit and forget the net; words are set for sense, catch the sense and forget the words. (*External Things*)

The net and fish trap are similes, what really requires expression is the meaning of words.

Zhuangzi harbored a deep distrust of speech, but if not through language, how can people communicate?

Laozi said: "The Way may be described in words but that Way is not constant; names may be named but those names are not constant." (*Chapter I*) He also said: "Those that know do not speak; those that speak do not know." (*Chapter LVI*) All this indicates that language cannot truly or sufficiently fulfil the role of transmission. However, the Tang dynasty poet Bai Juyi (772–846) questioned Laozi's statements saying: "Those who speak do not know and those who know are silent, this statement is said by Master Laozi; if Master Laozi were one of those who knew, what caused him to write 5,000 characters on it?" (*Reading Laozi*) In other words, "Laozi, you say yourself that it is difficult to convey meaning in words and furthermore that those who do so do not really 'know,' so why did you write those 5,000 words of *Laozi*?"

If Laozi and Zhuangzi were to reply they would probably say that although transmission through speech cannot be sufficient, true transmission will generate true sense and meaning. However, this is a path taken for the lack of anything better and as long as one does not stick stubbornly to this method, and pursues the basic aim of "sense" not "words" with clarity of mind, then "words are set for sense," the Way may be glimpsed through words and that's it. Once the sense has been grasped then words may be abandoned ("forget the words"), don't be immured in the text or entangled by the means. Imagine that it is a bridge that takes you across a river, you are across already but linger on the bridge—can you be reckoned to have truly crossed the river?

If you think the world a sea of mud, you cannot converse seriously

Nine out of ten fables take their examples from

elsewhere. A father cannot act as go-between in marriage for his own son. The recommendation of a father is not better than that of someone who is not the father. Any offence is not one's own but that of others. One accords with those who hold similar views and opposes those who do not. One approves similar views and denies dissimilar views. (*Fables*)

The story of the *kunpeng* transcends reality and is bizarre as well. The *kun* was originally just a fish, and then suddenly became the *peng* bird, which, if you think carefully is almost an act of transmutation, and this in itself is a consequence of the exercise of an extraordinary imagination. There is a similar story in the *Emperor* section of *Liezi*: "In the Ultimate North lies a dark sea, the Pool of Heaven. There is a fish of a width of 1,000 *li* with a length in proportion called a *kun*. There is a bird called a *peng* with wings like clouds in the sky with a body in proportion." However, in *Liezi*, there is no relationship of change between the *kun* and *peng*, in all probability the circumstances of change are the product of Zhuangzi's singular and fantastical imagination. Stories of the imagination contribute to an elevation of the spirit and transcend the purposes of the mundane world. Are they not precisely the archetypical fable?

The term "fable" is a creation from within *Zhuangzi* where there is a chapter of that title.

However, Zhuangzi's "fable" is not quite the same as the literary form that is understood as a fable today. Zhuangzi's fable is the borrowing of a topic as the basis for discussion of a separate issue, or using another subject for

the discussion of an idea that you wish to express yourself.
As later commentators explained it, "The meaning is *here*
but its expression is transferred over *there*." (Wang Xianqian,
Collected Commentaries on Zhuangzi) It is a case of wishing to
say something else but not doing so directly, rather along the
lines of "not my fault, it was somebody else." For example,
a father's praise of his son is not always accepted or believed
by others. "Of all scabby headed boys ours is the best," is
an expression of selfish favoritism, even of a narrowness
of mind that excludes anything different. In fact, if one's
son was truly outstanding where lies the harm in praise? It
is precisely because serious utterances often derive from
various kinds of inappropriate popular conceptions that they
so frequently fail to be accepted. Consequently, Zhuangzi
uses fables to express them: the world's a mess, you can't
talk properly—"If you think the world a sea of mud, you
cannot converse seriously." (*Beneath Heaven*)

At the time, fables were not just created for ease of
emotional and literary interest.

Treasure yourself

**The world laughs in scorn at those who use princely
pearls as pellets to shoot high-flying birds. Why?
Because the means are heavy and the gain slight.
(*Abdication*)**

This is Zhuangzi warning us to value our life and not to

lightly cast it away in pursuit of the valueless, such as glory, riches and status, rather as if using treasured pearls to shoot birds. There is also a universal significance here. So many people have discarded things that are truly worth cherishing merely for the sake of something regarded as of worldly value.

There is much in life that requires to be balanced out and for choices to be made. We must consider whether the aim is correct or not, is the price worth it? This is not the cultivation of a cunning sense of calculation but of self-worth.

Forgive the false hermit

Body amidst rivers and lakes but mind at court.
(*Abdication*)

In all the centuries of Chinese culture the hermit has never entirely disappeared like a wisp of smoke.

If we analyze a little, we can see that the circumstances of hermit-hood are quite complicated. There is true withdrawal and solitude and then there is false. The best hermits withdraw completely into the world of hills, forests and water, thereby disappearing without trace. Another esteemed kind of hermit was one (like the poet Tao Yuanming) for whom the intention of hermit-hood was no different from its reality:

Long caged in confinement,

Then to regain Nature once more.

Returning to Dwell amongst Fields and Gardens

Despite the many difficulties of rural life, in the end it was following one's inner nature, "rejoicing with heaven and understanding life" (*The Return*)—to be happy with one's lot. This was obviously genuine hermit-hood. False hermits were those with "body amidst rivers and lakes but mind at court." The most famous tale of a false hermit is known as "The short-cut by Mount Zhongnan."

The Tang dynasty poet Lu Cangyong (c. 664–c. 713) became a hermit during the reign of the Emperor Gaozong (649–683), but in the Zhongnan hills close to the capital Chang'an. Later, because the emperor was frequently at the eastern capital Luoyang, he found another hermit dwelling in the nearby Shaoshi hills. Thus, as the imperial carriage proceeded back and forth between the two capitals, so did Lu Cangyong travel to and fro between the Zhongnan and Shaoshi hills. The naked ambition of this "carriage trailing hermit" was well known. He eventually obtained preferment when Wu Zetian (624–705), the first empress in China, came to power and he descended from the hills to become an official. A well-known Daoist of the time, Sima Chengzhen (639–735) who was a hermit friend of Lu Cangyong, was once returning from Chang'an to the Zhongnan hills with him when Lu pointed to the hills and remarked: "These hills are truly a fine place, why go further!" Sima replied: "In my humble opinion they are a shortcut to office!" (Liu Su, *New Tales of the Tang—Hermits*)

Contempt apart, Zhuangzi was quite forgiving of this false Daoist of the Zhongnan short-cut. If false hermits were unable to restrain their worldly desires, then let them follow them; forced restraint would be a second injury and a second injury shortened life. In Zhuangzi's view, no matter what, preservation of life always took first place.

First cloud then rain at the flip of a hand

Those who take delight in praising others to their face will also delight in slandering them behind their backs. (Robber Zhi)

In the past, because of a tradition of humility, direct praise was a matter of embarrassment. A person who dared indulge in lavish praise face-to-face always aroused misgivings.

In his *Heaven and Earth* chapter Zhuangzi writes: "The filial son does not flatter his father nor the loyal minister his ruler, that is the glory of ministers and sons. When sons believe all their parents say to be true and all their actions to be virtuous, then they are commonly called unfilial. When ministers consider all their rulers say to be correct and all their actions to be benevolent, then they are commonly called unfaithful." In general, his main idea is that if sons are filial and ministers loyal then they should not flatter their fathers or their rulers. If, on the other hand, they generally just confirm their actions and behavior, then they are unfilial and disloyal. Their flattery and ingratiating behavior do not arise from sincerity but are often on account of self-interest rather than any true consideration of the interests of the father or the ruler. It may be called praise but it is enough to destroy them.

It was not only in the matter of face-to-face praise that their intentions were questionable. Since they were prepared to breach convention by indulging in it, there was also the considerable possibility of behind the scenes slander as well, and whether praise or slander, neither derived from any true intention but were determined by the requirements of advantage. Since it was possible, as it were, to present one's palm for cloud, then naturally one could also flip it over for rain; this was no obstacle to flatterers or slanderers, either in reality or psychologically.

From this we can see Zhuangzi's penetrating understanding of human emotions.

One joy a week

At the top man may live a hundred years, in the middle for eighty and at the bottom for sixty. Allowing for illness, deprivation, death, misery and suffering, the number of days available for laughter amount to a mere four or five a month. (*Robber Zhi*)

Zhuangzi's view of life was fundamentally pessimistic. There were matters beyond counting to be labored over, limitless responsibility to be fulfilled, immeasurable pressure to be accepted, and difficulties without number to be faced; for us there is no shortage of illness or injury or funerals, or of trouble to be taken. Man harbors hopeful expectations of a state of ease, of a mood of joy, but when all the unsatisfactory days are excluded, in the end it really looks as if there's not much time to be happy: "the number of days available for laughter amount to a mere four or five a month," that works out at, say, a day a week.

Zhuangzi's conclusion was quite prescient. In modern society one day of rest a week belongs to oneself, a time when it is comparatively easy to be content in oneself and to feel happy.

Undisturbed happiness

For heaven and earth there is no end, for man there is the time for death. If one were to place an entity with a sense of time in limitless space, then, suddenly, a life span would be the same as Qiji the wonder-horse flashing past a minute gap. Those who cannot achieve the joy they desire for the maintenance of life cannot understand the Way. (*Robber Zhi*)

Life has a limit and is over in a moment. The image of Qiji the wonder-horse appears not infrequently in *Zhuangzi*. In *Master Knowledge Travels North* there is "the life of man between heaven and earth is like the passage of the white colt across a tiny gap, suddenly over."

Faced with this fact, the question of how we should

confront it is something that only we ourselves can manage. Speaking in general, Zhuangzi proposes that one's natural life should be passed in tranquility but that, in the process, one should seek happiness to the utmost. Why inflict a grievance upon oneself?

However, there is a proper constraint here. In no way is Zhuangzi advocating just living for the pleasures of the present. To do so in the knowledge that everything passes and consequently to grasp every chance of present pleasure is the expression of a kind of decadence and despair as well as being a kind of arrogance. The joy of Zhuangzi is peaceful, undisturbed, like standing on a bridge and watching the fish so that self merges with matter in easy harmony.

The joy of the aspirations of one's heart lies in the nourishment of life and not in its indulgent dissipation.

Conceal shape and shadows disappear

There was a man who feared his shadow and loathed his footprints and sought to rid himself of them by running away. His footprints increased in number with every step he took and as fast as he went his shadow still kept up with him. He thought himself slow and hurried on without rest, exhausted his strength and died. He did not know that in shade his shadow would disappear and that at rest his footsteps would cease, what stupidity! (*The Fisherman*)

Zhuangzi was a sensitive man and sensitive people sometimes become obsessed by light and shadow. Zhuangzi referred to the relationship between shape and shadow a number of times. For example, in the *Treatise upon the Ordering of Things*, just before the final section, Zhuangzi's dream of being a butterfly, there is a conversation with a shadow in which the shadow says, "I don't know why I am always accompanied."

The circumstances surrounding escaping from a shadow seem of particular interest. Shadows move with shape, shape and shadow are inseparable, the elimination of traces can only be achieved at source, that is to say by "employing light to eliminate shade," if self does not shine with quite such brilliance, then shadow and trace will naturally fade. Put in current terms, one should empty self and mind and wander freely.

There is a passage in *Mountain Trees* about traveling by boat. "When traveling by boat on a river and an empty vessel strikes you, even the hottest tempered person is not angered. But if someone is aboard then you shout repeatedly. If the first shout is not heard, nor the second then at the third your frustration leads to bad language. From the previous absence of anger to present anger is the journey from the empty void to present reality. If man could empty the self and wander freely, who could harm him then?"

Emptying the self is not competing in the world outside, nor expending body and soul to no avail. To empty the self is to be as one entity with nature's great Way.

Truth lies not in form

Truth is the summation of sincerity. Without sincerity man cannot be moved. Hence those who weep forced tears may be sad but they are not grief-stricken, those who rage in forced anger may be stern but they lack power, those who profess forced friendship may smile but they are not kind. The truly sad grieve in silence, the truly angry hold back but are powerful, the truly friendly may not smile but are kind. (*The Fisherman*)

Truth is one of the most fundamental guiding principles of Daoism. To a certain extent it may be compared with the virtue (*shan*) of Confucianism.

Truth is the fundamental truth, the maintenance of the primal spiritual state, undistorted, without pretension, openly and sincerely. In this context, "forced" is the "forced" of the forced smile, an expression of falsehood, a pretense and thus incapable of moving anyone. The happiness, anger, sorrow and joy that arise from true emotion may not necessarily value external forms of expression. For example, can you say that the wailing of professional mourners proves that their grief is more profound than that of the mourners themselves?

Later on, Zhuangzi says: "One drinks wine for pleasure and mourns for grief"; hence the drinking of wine is on account of the pursuit of pleasure, thus there is no need to be particular about the drinking vessel. Equally, mourning is on account of grief, thus there is no need to be particular about ceremony.

Ruan Ji (210–263), one of the Seven Worthies of the

Bamboo Grove who lived during the Wei and Jin dynasties (220–420), might be termed a model for the practice of this "truth." The biography of Ruan Ji in the *History of the Jin* says of him, "He was by nature most filial, when his mother passed away he was engaged in a game of chess (*wei qi*), his opponent sought an end to the game but he did not reply. He then drank two measures (*dou*) of wine, gave a great cry and vomited much blood. At the funeral he ate roast suckling pig and drank two measures of wine and at the final parting he cried out and yet again vomited much blood, his flesh shriveled and his bones protruded so that he was on the point of death."

Ruan Ji looks like a man not much given to the niceties of ceremonial etiquette. His mother dies but he carries on playing chess and he eats flesh and drinks wine, but there can be no doubt that his feelings are absolutely genuine. His grief is not expressed through adherence to the rites of a worldly funeral; the external changes in appearance brought about by shriveled flesh and protruding bones reveals the utmost heartbreak and despair and are Zhuangzi's core sense of the idea of mourning in practice.

Consequently, external forms are unimportant, the crux lies in the essential substance of the inner mind.

Better to go without a funeral

I take heaven and earth for my coffin, sun and moon for my amulet, stars for my beads and all living things as

**grave goods. How can my funeral accoutrements not be
ready? (*Lie Yukou*)**

In theory, Zhuangzi had a clear awareness of the problems
of life and death. However, in the end, theory and practice
are two very different things, many people think but do
nothing. Zhuangzi's "drumming on a bowl and singing" (on
the death of his wife) may be considered the single act of
practice of a lifetime. Nevertheless, something that involves
someone else (even the wife who has lived with you for half
a lifetime) is very different from something that involves
oneself. So many people possess clarity when a bystander
but are at a loss when involved themselves.

The clear-headed loyalty to his own ideas that Zhuangzi
displayed as he faced his final destination is truly convincing.
He rejected the plans for an elaborate funeral that his
disciples had made with the statement above, utterly natural
in his own eyes but shocking to others. The exchange that
followed was even more disturbing. The disciples said: "We
fear that you will become food for the birds." Zhuangzi
replied: "As between being eaten by birds above, or
devoured by ants beneath, where is the difference between
one or the other?"

Zhuangzi's attitude stood beyond normal sense, but it
is actually the natural consequence of the thorough practice
of his ideas on life and death. Moreover, in point of practical
experience, Zhuangzi was rather clever. There were no
good consequences to an elaborate funeral. The historical
commentaries of the Miscellaneous School, compiled on
the eve of Qin Shihuang's unification of China as *Lu's Spring*

and Autumn Annals, contain a chapter with the title *Peaceful Death*: it says that an inscription on a tomb tells the world that precious jewels lie beneath and will be laughed at. Isn't this the same as an elaborate funeral? "From times ancient to the present there have never been states that have not fallen, to be without states that have not fallen is to be without tombs that have not been dug up." Then what about simple funerals?

The last testaments of Zhang Qi (d. 1048) of the Song dynasty and the poet Yan Shu (991–1055) were very different. Zhang chose an elaborate funeral and Yan a simple one. Later, grave robbers recovered a rich haul from Zhang's grave but did not break into the coffin and unable to take it away they withdrew. Yan's tomb contained only a score or two of pottery vessels, the robbers expended a great deal of energy with no return for their labors and in a fit of rage smashed the great poet's bones to smithereens. (Shao Wen in *Reminiscences of the Shao Clan—Shaoshi wenjian houlu*)

If an elaborate funeral is no good and there are unforeseen dangers to a simple one, then it would be better to have no funeral at all!

Dates of the Chinese Dynasties

Xia Dynasty	2070–1600 BC
Shang Dynasty	1600–1046 BC
Zhou Dynasty	1046–256 BC
Western Zhou Dynasty	1046–771 BC
Eastern Zhou Dynasty	770–256 BC
Spring and Autumn Period	770–476 BC
Warring States Period	475–221 BC
Qin Dynasty	221–206 BC
Han Dynasty	206 BC–AD 220
Western Han Dynasty	206 BC–AD 25
Eastern Han Dynasty	25–220
Three Kingdoms	220–280
Wei	220–265
Shu Han	221–263
Wu	222–280
Jin Dynasty	265–420
Western Jin Dynasty	265–316
Eastern Jin Dynasty	317–420
Northern and Southern Dynasties	420–589
Southern Dynasties	420–589
Northern Dynasties	439–581
Sui Dynasty	581–618
Tang Dynasty	618–907
Five Dynasties and Ten Kingdoms	907–960
Five Dynasties	907–960
Ten Kingdoms	902–979
Song Dynasty	960–1279
Northern Song Dynasty	960–1127
Southern Song Dynasty	1127–1279
Liao Dynasty	916–1125
Jin Dynasty	1115–1234
Xixia Dynasty (or Tangut)	1038–1227
Yuan Dynasty	1279–1368
Ming Dynasty	1368–1644
Qing Dynasty	1644–1911

Index to Chapters of *Zhuangzi*

Text by Zhuangzi
Commentary by Chen Yinchi
Translation by Tony Blishen

Design by Wang Wei
Cover Photo by CFP

Copy Editor: Diane Davies
Assistant Editor: Qiu Yan
Editor: Wu Yuezhou

ISBN: 978-1-93836-891-2

Address any comments about *The Way to Inner Peace* to:

SCPG
401 Broadway, Ste. 1000
New York, NY 10013
USA

or

Shanghai Press and Publishing Development Co., Ltd.
Floor 5, 390 Fuzhou Road, Shanghai, China (200001)
Email: sppd@sppdbook.com

Printed in China by Shanghai Donnelley Printing Co., Ltd.
1   3   5   7   9   10   8   6   4   2